Best wishes

Bill Kreml

t/5/17

The Bias of Temperament in American Politics

The Bias of Temperament in American Politics

Second Edition

William P. Kreml

CAROLINA ACADEMIC PRESS
Durham, North Carolina

Library of Congress Cataloging-in-Publication Data

Kreml, William P.
The bias of temperament in American politics / William P.
Kreml. -- Second edition.
    pages cm
Includes bibliographical references and index.
ISBN 978-1-61163-544-7 (alk. paper)
1. Political psychology--United States. I. Title.

JA74.5.K717 2014
320.97301'9--dc23

2013044081

Carolina Academic Press
700 Kent Street
Durham, North Carolina 27701
Telephone (919) 489-7486
Fax (919) 493-5668
www.cap-press.com

To
Mark Whittington
A Great South Carolinian
A Great American

At its best, the left foretells the future.
At its worst, it misunderstands the past.

Contents

Acknowledgments

I wish to thank my friend Alexander Moore who twice read a draft of this piece and made useful comments, particularly regarding the sequencing of chapters. A hearty thanks to my publisher, Keith Sipe, for his unflinching support of a work that is somewhat off his company's usual script. Finally, my thanks to Nancy Mace Kreml whose editorial assistance is exceeded only by her steadfast and caring support. Any remaining errors are my responsibility alone.

Introduction

Not long ago, I attended a talk given by the noted author and social critic Barbara Ehrenreich at Chicago's Newberry Library. The bulk of her talk concerned the plight of the poor and the plight of women. It was a good presentation, but I was happily surprised when Ms. Ehrenreich did not conclude with the above themes. Near the close of her talk, she spent a few moments discussing something that I had never heard her speak of or write about before, something I thought was important.

Beyond the myriad of discriminations against the poor and women, she offered, there was a further discrimination in the private sector regarding hiring, pay, promotion, job allocation, and the like. That discrimination was based on personality. It was a discrimination that grew out of many employers' use of the standard Myers-Briggs personality inventory to find if and where a potential employee might fit in. This test, created during World War II, grew out of the Jungian introversion-extroversion dichotomy. Ms. Ehrenreich related how private corporations overwhelmingly discriminate against those who demonstrated introverted personality traits in favor of those who demonstrated extroverted traits. More recently, Susan Cain has written *Quiet*, a compelling work that explores examples of how the extrovertive personality is favored over the introvertive personality in a variety of American occupational, educational, and social venues. I confess I had not thought very much about such biases in the context of the private domain. I have long suspected, and have written about, how this kind of discrimination occurred in the public sector, with attendant consequences in public policy, as well as in the very design of the structures and processes of the American government.

Let me be clear about what I am doing in this short work. Roughly one third of this piece is unabashedly a summary of writings that can be found in other places, generally in books and articles that I have written over the years. The burden of these writings was to describe an original political philosophy, one based upon psychology rather than economics, or any other objective reality. The theory borrows, among other places, from a) the sub-atomic intellectual framework of the Danish physicist Niels Bohr and the English Ernest Rutherford, b) the introversion-extroversion psychological continuum of Carl Jung, and c) a comparison of the kinds of minds of the two great German Idealist thinkers, Immanuel Kant and G. W. F. Hegel.

I have written on this topic over the years because I have become convinced that, outrageous though some of the manifestations of traditional bias continue to be, the greatest bias in American politics may no longer be against groups like African-Americans, women, gays and lesbians, or the like. I believe that the greatest bias in American politics might now be a bias of temperament. The most discriminated-against group in the body politic may no longer be an ethnic group, or even an economic group, or something similar. The most discriminated against of American citizens might well be found *within* all of the traditionally spoken of groups that are part of the American political mosaic. This citizenry is made up of the population that is psychologically introspective, as Ms. Ehrenreich, Susan Cain, and, of course, those like Carl Jung have articulated it. Further, that population has a preference for synthetic cognitive forms, or the apples and oranges kind of knowledge, as Kant and Hegel, although very differently, grappled with such forms.

What an original political theory based upon psychology offers, therefore, is something altogether different from what other political theories offer. If we revere the humane political contributions of figures like Mohandas Gandhi, the Reverend Martin Luther King, Jr., Nelson Mandela, or even a figure from long ago like Saint Francis of Assisi, why do we not revere the contributions of far less substantial figures, ordinary people like you and I, who are of the temperament of the above figures, if not of their stature?

Why, in short, do we not recognize the contribution of those whose temperaments contribute in far more humble settings, often in the role of a personal mediator and/or in the role of cementing the bonds within a group, or in being the reconciler of interests, all accomplished in a balance with those of a more competitive, more individualistic temperament? Finally, why do we not recognize the contributions of the temperament that prefers the kind of political structures and processes which facilitate the amelioration of conflict and embrace the public good over the splintered, selfish demands of powerful private interests?

At root, all political theory rests on a standard of equity. Like the rest of any citizenry that is even mildly left of center in its political orientation, I have vigorously endorsed, marched for, and contributed to the movements that supported equity for African-Americans, women, LGBT citizens, the poor, the under paid, soldiers in an unnecessary war, and other discriminated against groups all my life. But note that the above list of the aggrieved was invariably discriminated against on the basis of some objective criteria — that is, on some other-than-mind-based, or subjective, quality. Again, I have long supported, and will always support, those so often justified pleas. But I submit, much like Ms. Ehrenreich and Ms. Cain, that something else is also going on. Once again, I think it goes on, and has gone on, every bit as much in the public as in the private sector.

In the United States, if not in other places in short, there is a political bias that has not yet been dealt with, a bias that not only affects those who suffer the discrimination but even more importantly contributes to the building and maintenance of an imbalanced political system and the creation of its unjust political outcomes. I am hardly the only citizen who believes that the American political system is badly out of balance. The political philosophy that I have attempted to create over many years rests on an intellectual foundation that I hope will expose and lead to the effective correction of such imbalances. I broach the costs of not engaging in what I immodestly think of as a Niels Bohr-like sub-atomic revolution in political thought. We who work in politics, and write about politics, are well behind the physicists and their sub-atomic theory. Maybe it is time that this social science, as well as the real world of politics, catch up a bit with the hard scientists. I think we can do that in politics with a theory I call the Natural, or Psychological, Left.

This work is divided into three parts and an epilogue. The first part, made up of seven minimalist chapters, describes the theory. The second part, of three longer chapters, places the theory into what I hope is a deeper intellectual and political context. Part three's five chapters apply the theory to the American political system as well as to a schema that describes religious history, all containing what I believe to be original diagnoses of cognitively based political imbalances. The epilogue specifically discusses the structural biases of our country's political structures, and makes specific, in some cases constitutional, recommendations for change. And yes, the argument is rather simply dichotomous, but so is digital and this should be only a beginning.

Part One

The Theory

Chapter One

The Psychology of Politics

The genesis of my interest in the psychology of why people believe what they believe politically rests vividly in my memory. That interest began in Chicago, late at night specifically, and always on the weekends. During the nineteen fifties and early sixties, two Chicago television channels hosted live roundtable programs on which public figures hashed out their positions concerning a variety of political subjects. One of the shows was hosted by the noted Chicago *Sun-Times* columnist, Irv Kupcinet. The other was hosted by John Madigan, another local journalist. I watched them much later into the night than I should have, their shows frequently running until three in the morning. I found that I simply could not go to bed.

The guests on these shows were varied in their backgrounds and ideologies, although curiously I only specifically remember one individual. He was the conservative William Rusher, the man who helped found and then published *The National Review* which, under the editorship of the late William F. Buckley, Jr., became America's leading conservative organ. I remember Rusher for a simple reason: although the two above hosts seemed to have no trouble finding a smorgasbord of liberal-to-left thinkers on all kinds of topics over the weeks, it became clear that conservatives found sitting up and arguing with liberals into the night to be somehow less appealing. Rusher, it seemed, was on one of the two shows almost every other week. I did not agree with him on very much, but I did admire his tenacity.

While I learned a great deal from these programs about the contemporary issues of the day, I found that I was, perhaps more intuitively than anything else, learning something beyond politics as well. One theme that recurred in my thinking became increasingly haunting: although I enjoyed the arguments of the participants greatly, I was increasingly frustrated by the fact that these lengthy and well-informed political figures never, and I mean never, came to a resolution of their disputes. At no point in their discussions, particularly near the close where it might have been expected, did anyone utter "By gosh, you're right" or "You've convinced me." Instead, what became clear was that the participants all wound up the program exactly where they had begun, not only in terms of their specific positions on any political issue, but in their foundational political ideologies as well. These people clearly valued different things, at a very deep level. Just as surely, as I slowly discovered, they even thought differently about these things in some mechanical way that I did not yet fully understand. It was only a resultant reality that they differed on the issues.

In short, what became clear to me was that the participants who called themselves conservative and took conservative political positions, including Mr. Rusher, as well as the participants who called themselves liberal and took liberal political positions, not only differed at the level of their substantive politics. There was a deeper difference here, a difference, if I may, in the very forms, or structures of their thinking, or ultimately of *how* rather than what, the participants thought about things. They seemed, perhaps, to have different kinds of minds. That was what I remember starting to think about as a late night watcher of these political arguments.

This early detection of a difference in the very forms of how various political advocates thought became the foundation for what I have been attempting to do with an original theory over the years. There were differences between those who would regulate private business and those who would leave things to the market, or differences between those who would attempt to balance employer-to-employee salary negotiations and those who would not, and even differences between those who would favor or not favor governmental activism in, say, the protection of the environment. Most importantly, the reason for these differences was all a part of something else. It was only from a growing understanding of the roots of these differences that I began to develop a theory based on the psychological, mostly cognitive, nature of different human minds.

My interest in the psychology of politics continued to grow throughout my formal education. I reached another plateau with the reading of the early psychology and politics writings of Harold Lasswell, Emory Bogardus, Graham Wallas, and, most importantly, the post-Holocaust study of T.W. Adorno, Else-Frenkel Brunswick, Daniel Levinson, Nevitt Sanford, and others. These Frankfurt School authors, mostly of a Marxist bent, put together a number of research articles in the classic *The Authoritarian Personality*. Their findings described psychological predispositions, or traits, that tended to correlate with anti-democratic, even autocratic, political structures, as well as dictatorial political figures. The Berkeley work, as it came to be known because of its publication by the University of California Press, created a variety of personality scales, including the E-scale, for ethnocentrism, the PEC scale, for political and economic conservatism, the A-S scale for anti-Semitism, and, most significantly, the F-scale, an inventory that tested for fascist, or perhaps better, pre-fascist personality characteristics.

The F-scale was not without faults, and it was legitimately criticized by many conservative scholars. Surely, it included a variety of unpleasant psychological traits that did not exclusively correlate with right-wing political attitudes in the category of the pre-fascist. Dogmatism, after all, could occur at any point on the psycho-political spectrum, and probably most frequently at both extremes rather than exclusively on the right, as a researcher like Milton Rokeach pointed out. Further, the F-scale definitions of what did and what did not constitute democratic political views had more than a little leftist tilt to them. But, after all was said and done, the F-Scale still seemed to identify a number of core psychological orientations that portended the holding of extreme right-wing views.

To be sure, *The Authoritarian Personality* and instruments like the F-scale did not articulate a political theory. Yet, at the same time, I felt that they did point the way to a theory. Although there was but brief mention of an anti-authoritarian personality and a correspondingly left political position in the over one thousand pages, *TAP* did not establish correlations between specific personality traits and their attendant political orientations across the *entire* spectrum of political-to-psychological linkages. Put another way, there was no completed, that is full-spectrum, psycho-political range in *TAP*, and there was no theory based on the notion of providing for the equitable input of all personalities in *TAP* either.

The above omission essentially defined my own research. Soon after, I wrote a doctoral dissertation which, with some further massaging, became my first book: *The Anti-Authoritarian Personality*. Using various scaling techniques, I tried to demonstrate that the four core authoritarian personality characteristics of a) a high need for power, b) a high need for order, c) a need to repress impulse, and d) a tendency towards extroversion, were the core of right-leaning ideologies. Further, the holders of those characteristics' correlation with right of center political attitudes were matched at the other end of the psycho-political spectrum with those who evidenced a) a low need for power, b) a low need for order, c) a willingness to vent impulse, and d) a generally introverted personality. Incomplete though my early research surely was, I believe it offered at least some evidence for the proposition that there was a full spectrum relationship between individual psychologies and political ideology. For me, that full-spectrum relationship would serve as the catalyst for a political theory based upon human personality.

References

T. W. Adorno, et al. *The Authoritarian Personality,* New York, Harper and Row, 1950.

Susan Cain, *Quiet,* Crown Publishers, New York, 2012.

W. P. Kreml, *The Anti-Authoritarian Personality,* London, Pergamon Press, 1977.

Milton Rokeach, *The Open and Closed Mind,* New York, Basic Books, 1960.

Chapter Two

The Analytic and
Synthetic Cognitions

The psychological variables I described in the first chapter are generally known as affective variables. Affective variables, such as those dealing with the need for power, the need for order, etc., describe human feelings and would be necessary for any psychologically based theory, of course. But I soon concluded that they alone were not sufficient. No robust psychological theory of politics could base itself solely on feelings. There had to be something else, and that something, I soon discovered, had to be cognitive, that is dealing with the way, or the very forms, of how people think.

At its simplest level, cognition defines the mental maps that each of us use to help organize our thoughts. Years before the writing of my dissertation, I had written my master's thesis on what I thought were the significant psychological differences between Thomas Jefferson and Alexander Hamilton. In retrospect, I think that much of what I described there was cognitive as well as affective. Is it any wonder, when you think of it, that we remember Jefferson for things like his being the principal creator of the ringing Declaration of Independence, as well as for his glorious architecture, while we remember Hamilton for his masterful comprehension of things like public credit and mercantilist economic productivity? Underlying the left-to-right spectral differences between these polar titans of American liberalism and conservatism, I thought, were significant psychological differences. I decided that I would pursue the cognitive variable further as the principal underpinning for a psychologically based theory.

But where should I go, I wondered, to find the philosophical raw material for a cognitive psychological variable? In searching for a philosophical foundation for a psychologically based theory, I recalled the discussions of cognitions within the writings of the two German Idealist thinkers, Immanuel Kant and G. W. F. Hegel. Like many before them, they had written themselves about the "forms" of knowledge, or the shapes that various kinds of knowledge take, quite apart from their substance. Of course, Plato had written of the forms in the *Phaedo*. Leonardo wrote of the forms and inventively argued that painting represented the forms even better than sculpture. Michelangelo strongly disagreed. André Malraux had returned time and again to the forms when he portrayed the progression of Western art. But it was Kant and Hegel who became essential to my theory because the very different manner in which each of them classified forms of knowledge seemed to reveal their very different kinds of minds.

In this work, I will use the two classical terms, analytic and synthetic, to describe what is commonly understood to be the apples and apples relationship (analytic) versus the apples and oranges relationship (synthetic). A richer philosophical understanding than that exists, of course, these categories having been around for a long time and, within the formalities of philosophy, having to do with things like the subjects and predicates of sentences. But we don't need that complication here. Let us just think of the differences between Kant's and Hegel's minds, not wholly unlike the differences between Hamilton's and Jefferson's minds incidentally, as being best revealed in the two philosophers' analytic versus synthetic definitions of the mathematical equation $7 + 5 = 12$. Kant had depicted this equation as being synthetic in its form, like the comparison of apples and oranges. He argued that since there were two numbers on one side of the equation and only one on the other, $7 + 5 = 12$ was therefore a synthetic statement. Hegel differed. He argued that the most significant characteristic of the equation was that 5, 7, and 12 were all numbers, and that the equation was therefore analytic, containing only like, not unlike, variables. For Hegel, $7 + 5 = 12$ was not a synthetic statement. To him, both sides of the equation were numbers, so the equation was of the apples and apples form.

Why did Kant and Hegel differ over the correct designation of the $7 + 5 = 12$ definition? The answer, I suggest, is not difficult to discern. A mind like Kant's, I submit, prefers the analytic cognition and will register almost any variance of cognitive quality as synthetic. A mind like Hegel's that naturally prefers the synthetic cognition, in contrast, will require a significant cognitive differentiation (a considerable apples to oranges differentiation) in order to classify a proposition as synthetic.

Also, if one looks at how the two different cognitive categories were used by Kant and Hegel within a variety of philosophical contexts, one finds that Hegel's preference for the synthetic cognition is evident in his perspective on the reach of speculative philosophy, or metaphysics, the dialectic, or even considerations concerning the nature of knowledge itself. Hegel held to his preferences in these arenas because he had a synthetic, speculative, or non-linear, kind of mind. I disagree, incidentally, with Hegel's contention that the synthetic cognition is a superior cognition than the analytic cognition. My position is that neither cognition is inherently superior to the other, and that the holders of any one cognition, the subjects of our inquiry, should not be preferred over another within any polity. I do believe, however, that the synthetic cognition, and those who prefer that cognition as it is the natural product of their mind, has generally been minimized within the American political experience. If one is intent on building a political theory based on a standard of cognitive equity as that equity impacts the citizens of any polity, the two grand cognitive forms must be granted equal political status.

It should not be a surprise that Kant, in contrast to Hegel, preferred the analytic to the synthetic cognitive form, something that squares with a great deal of evidence that Kant had a linear, deductive, or analytic mind. All things being equal, Kant's mind preferred similar variables, again the apples and apples form, and his notions concerning metaphysics, the dialectic, and the nature of knowledge itself were, accordingly, very different from Hegel's. Kant's concern with the categorization of knowledge, as well as his highly restrictive sense of the dialectic's ability consciously to move history, starkly contrasted with Hegel's more expansive metaphysics. Central to any psychologically based political philosophy is an understanding of such cognitively based predispositions, and of how such predispositions impact things like the relative political favor for public sector regulation of the private sector, or the relative favor for frankly redistributive, progressive taxation.

A final point. Again, the theory that I am describing is subjectively based. It deals with the mind, in the first instance separated from the objective world. Objectively-based political theories have been grounded in the world outside the mind, their starting point resting in social and economic standing, class, gender, race, ability, and other objectivities. A subjectively based political theory need never deny the importance of these realities. But this theory will focus on the internal mental and emotional states that interpret the external world. The importance of the subjective variable does not in any way vitiate the continued importance of the objective, or real world, within all ideologies and all contemporary political considerations. All of us are of a social and economic class, a race, a gender, a region, a sexual disposition, and so forth. These pre-political identifications we will always have with us.

What I am suggesting in building a psychologically based theory that may have relevance in an economically developed polity like that of the United States is that the subjective variable has become ever more important over the last years because the cognitive proclivity for different ways of thinking exists within each objective political category at the same time that it transcends all objective categories. This circumstance permits, in fact it requires, the building of a political theory based upon a new, subjective, understanding. Latino female citizens, or African-American males, all things equal, will evidence a full range of cognitive differentiation.

How do we know that the subjective variable holds sway in a country like the United States? Well, have you noticed that whereas the working class overwhelmingly used to vote Democratic, Ronald Reagan's position on a variety of social and cultural issues encouraged many of them to begin to vote Republican, where their loyalties now frequently remain? And have you noticed that whereas most Baptists used to vote Democratic, since they were often of the working class, and most Episcopalians, frequently more upscale, tended to vote Republican, these allegiances have substantially reversed over the last generation of American elections? Most

Baptists are simply more orthodox in their personal, or ethical, values then are the often more socially liberal Episcopalians. These sub-atomic examples are byproducts of subjectively based ideological identifications. If we can understand why things like this have happened, then I think we can begin to define a standard of equity within a theoretically subjective context that responds to the current bias in favor of the extrovertive personality and its forms of understanding the world that exists in the American political system.

References

G. W. F. Hegel, *The Phenomenology of Mind,* London, George Allen and Unwin, 1966.

Leonardo, *The Italian Renaissance,* ed. Werner L. Gundersheimer, Englewood Cliffs, Prentice-Hall, 1965.

Andre Malraux, *The Human Adventure,* trans. Violet M. Horvath, New York, New York University Press, 1969.

Plato, *The Phaedo of Plato,* ed. R. D. Archer-Hind, New York: Arno Press, 1973.

William E. Wallace, *Michelangelo: The Complete Sculpture, Painting, Architecture,* Hugh Lauter Levin, Westport, 1998.

Yirmiahu Yovel, *Kant and the Philosophy of History,* Princeton, Princeton University Press, 1980.

Chapter Three

Reversing the Analytic Bias

As before, the original political theory I offer here is probably best called a theory of the Natural, or Psychological, Left. It is different from those traditional political theories that are based upon legal and political arrangements, such as classical liberalism, or upon economic arrangements, such as the various shades of modern liberalism, or socialism. Classical liberalism began with the individual and a set of rights, originally with such civil rights as the ability to own property and sell (alienate) that property free of feudal restrictions. The growth of what were called civil rights into economic rights, such as the right to be served in public accommodations or to have an equal shot at a job, grew again into social rights such as the right to be educated in non-segregated schools, and then into political rights like the right to vote. The above were all natural extensions of the liberal promise.

In contrast with liberal theory, economically based theories initiated the consideration of groups, specifically objectively defined whole groups like the working class. Objectively based theories grew from there, appropriately seeking to grant legal and political equality to women, or gays and lesbians in the legal state of marriage, or other groups that had not been equitably treated.

In this chapter, I will attempt to describe the three conceptual bulwarks that underpin a psychologically, specifically cognitively, based theory of politics. They are 1) the sub-atomic nature of the theory, 2) the necessary distinction between the objective and the subjective ideological variable, and 3) the necessary return to the classical, that is Plato-to-Hegel, Idealistic Dialectic. This latter bulwark imports the necessary turning away from the Materialist Dialectic which, even without the specifics of Marx or Marxism, still overshadows much of the political thinking that defines individuals, and whole groups, solely by their material condition.

As an overarching concept, a sub-atomic theory, therefore, argues that *for every objectivity, there is a subjectivity.* Put another way, what a sub-atomic theory insists on is that within the dichotomy of things of the mind and things of the objective world, there is a relationship between the subjective and the objective which finds that your being, say, an Illinois female, tells us nothing about what kind of mind you have. Whether you are wealthy or poor, gay or straight, of one racial category or another, in other words, tells us nothing about whether you are an extrovert or an introvert, to use Jung's classifications, or whether you incline towards the analytic kind of mind or the synthetic kind of mind, to use the cognitive preferences that were so evident in the thinking of Kant and Hegel. Whether you have a mind like Jefferson's or Hamilton's, for example, may have a good deal to do with whether you have a cognitive inclination in favor of synthetically formed intrusions into something like a private contract. I use the contract example deliberately, incidentally, as I will say a good deal more on the matter of contracts and their encumbrances later.

What this theory suggests, therefore, is that unless there has been some significant, even if wholly unintentional, separation of different personalities within various objective groups, all objectively defined political groupings will contain the entire range of subjectivities. What a sub-atomic theory also suggests is that we are now at that point in history where the admittedly still incomplete successes of whole objective groups like workers, Latinos, etc. portend the arrival of what I call the "sub-atomic" political moment. The political sub-atomic moment occurs when the subjective, cognitively based political orientations of a citizenry begin to outweigh objectively based orientations.

As a result of the coming of the sub-atomic moment, or the ascendance of the subjective over the objective as I began to suggest in the last chapter, the lessons of the sub-atomic physicist Niels Bohr can be borrowed, within a philosophical context, as a metaphor for an equitable placement of cognitions *inside* the structures and processes of public institutions. Only if that is done, I suggest, will we have a more equitable polity than the mere enhancement of the condition of heretofore discriminated against objective groups can ever bring. In sum, as I said at the outset, even with all of the un-finished agendas of the African-American community, women, and the like, the most significant political discrimination in an eco-nomically advanced society like the United States in the twenty-first century may increasingly be the discrimination against those of a cognitively synthetic personality, such personality, again, lying within all objective classifications. Again, *for every objectivity, there is a subjectivity.*

Correspondingly, I suggest that the above subjectively based political discrimination will only be apparent when it is placed into the context of a political theory that describes how the fair inclusion of all citizens does nothing to prevent the dominance of those of the analytic over the synthetic cognition *within* contexts like, say, the internal arrangements of the United States Congress. The dispersion of committees, subcommittees, and a variety of centrifugal arrangements that grew out of the so-called reforms of the 1970s, I would suggest, have done great harm to America's federal legislature.

Over time, does one cognitive form triumph over another within the typical organizational setting, be it in the private or public sec-tor? I will only quickly refer here to the vast literature in fields like organizational theory that demonstrate the triumph, over time, of the analytic over the synthetic cognition within all organizations. From Robert Michels' "Iron Law of Oligarchy," describing how sub-components within institutions divide and insulate themselves, through Anthony Downs' notions of the organizational "zealot" who is loyal only to "narrow concepts or policies," to Howard Aldrich's notions of the role of "boundary personnel" who protect sub-jurisdictions within institutions because they are the person-alities most adept at creating and preserving insulated prerogatives, the "personality sort" (my term) within virtually all structures has been well documented. That personality sort requires an under-standing of the "sub-atomic" character of psychological types and a compensatory (synthetic over analytic) readjustment of impor-tant public institutions like the Congress. The "sort" also requires us to maintain a cognitive understanding of how institutions like congressional committees might maintain their primary commitment to the public good, and not to narrow, powerful interests.

Put another way, it will make little difference over time if a political entity achieves a balance of women, blacks, gays and lesbians, etc. in its institutions, something I surely endorse and have been happy to see improvement on in the United States, if the cognitive preferences of those objectively favored individuals are skewed in such a way that those institutions, and the policy output of those institutions, still yield inequitable results. The fact is that at a time when the representation of minorities, women, and so many other groupings within our politics has partially succeeded, as evidenced by the presidential campaigns of Democratic Party figures like Senators Hillary Clinton and Barack Obama, the distribution of income and wealth in this country continues to deteriorate as salaries, worker hours, loss of retirement benefits, and similar distributional benchmarks only get worse.

Put still another way, as the influence of powerful, largely corporate, lobbies has grown, and as such measures as the decline of the percentage of federal taxes that are paid by corporations continues, the aggregated voice of the general populace justifiably feels left out of the political process. If we do not achieve a Niels Bohr-like sub-atomic breakthrough, and if we do not simultaneously achieve a subjectively-based representative equity in America's public institutional makeup, the above inequities, and so many more, will never be corrected. Let me be clear: by all means the commitment to the African-American and other minority ethnic communities, the feminist community, the LGBT community, and all other objectively based communities, must continue. But it is time for the next step. It is time to move beyond these objective categories to an even more refined set of principles that offer a precise, and more powerful, guarantee of political equity to the American people. If Barbara Ehrenreich-like discrimination in the private sector is to be corrected in the public sector, this must be done.

In the final analysis, do not forget, cognitive balance within America's political structures will still benefit those objective groups that legitimately make their claim to equity. If within every objective group there is a full subjective range of analytic to synthetic minds, then the internal balance of these subjectivities within political institutions is not only the best guarantee of sub-atomic equity within the political system, but it is also the best guarantee that the "out groups" of society, which a synthetic mind pays proper attention to, will always be considered.

To better see where the inequity of psychologies relates to the very forms of governments, we will shortly examine the classic Aristotelian trichotomy of governmental forms that includes the one, the few, and the many. We will see where the imbalance of the analytic cognition over the synthetic cognition impacts this classical paradigm. But we will understand the Aristotelian trichotomy of governmental forms far better, I suggest, if we look first at a) the relationship of the subjective and the objective ideological spectra, b) the necessary return to the Idealist over the Materialist dialectic and c) the cognitive form of the dialectic itself. I shall discuss each of these matters in the following three short chapters. Then we will turn to the cognitively generated revision of Aristotle's classical trichotomy.

References

Howard Aldrich, *Organization and Environments,* Englewood Cliffs, Prentice-Hall, 1979.

Anthony Downs, *Inside Bureaucracy,* Boston, Little Brown, 1967.

Carl Jung, *Psychological Types,* London, trans. H. Godwin Baynes, Routledge and Kegan Paul, 1923.

Robert Michels, *Political Parties: A Sociological Study of the Oligarchical Tendencies of Modern Democracy,* New York, Dover Publications, 1957.

Chapter Four

Objective and
Subjective Ideologies

America's need for both a sub-atomic psycho-political bench-mark and a sub-atomically derived rebalancing of our political institutions requires a sound theoretical grounding within a psychologically-based political philosophy. To build that philosophy, we should first deal with the interrelationship of the objective and the subjective variables themselves. Imagine two horizontal lines that represent political spectra. One is objective and the other subjective. The objective or ideological spectrum is already fairly well understood. It runs from the far right, with extremist ideologies like fascism and its most horrid manifestation National Socialism, to the far left, with the kind of radical communism that even Lenin found abhorrent. The subjective spectrum is what we are developing, including the relative need for order and power etc. of affective variables and, more centrally here, the analytic-to-synthetic range of cognitive variables.

It may be fair to say that on the right, the two spectra, the objective and the subjective, are more or less parallel. The absolutist, highly orthodox ideologies, and the need for order and power, along with the impulse suppression and extroversion that is also found with those of affectively authoritarian personality traits, translate into authoritarian and ethnocentric regimes. Cognitively, these ideologies attract, and draw strength from, the highly analytic mind, that is the mind that finds it more difficult to meld the qualitative mix of ethnicities, cultures, languages, and the like that go with a benign, liberal (in the original meaning), political society. At the same time, the structures and processes of these polity's governments are almost invariably centralized in their organization, at the same time that they are rigid, dictatorial, and repressive of oppositional input.

Moving across the spectrum, the centrist ideologies that gently dominate the planet's true democracies evidence a balance of both affective and cognitive psychological variables, along with an equitable balance of the centralizing and decentralizing forces within political structures, political processes, and a resultant balance of public policy. But when one continues much beyond this mid-point, moving to the left, something dramatic begins to happen. As we proceed to the left along the two spectra, we come to a place where the objective spectrum diverges from the subjective spectrum, and eventually begins to move in the opposite direction. The extreme objective left eventually corresponds to the subjective right.

To visualize this, let us go to the other end of the psychological spectrum, all the way to what I call the Natural, or Psychological Left. It is there that you find Mohandas Gandhi, the Reverend Martin Luther King, Jr., Mother Teresa, Nelson Mandela, or the Czech satirical playwright Vaclav Havel and the Czech satirical novelist Jaroslav Hašek (*The Good Soldier Schweik*). It is there that you won't find Joseph Stalin, Mao Zedong, Pol Pot, or Kim Jung Il. These latter kinds of authoritarians, though objectively left in their politics, clearly reside on the other end of the subjective spectrum from the Natural Left figures. In fact, their political leadership, and the highly centralized political structures and processes that they typically employ, bear a striking resemblance to the politics of someone like Adolf Hitler, or other dictators of the far right such the late General Augusto Pinochet of Chile, or the recently "reelected" Robert Mugabe in Zimbabwe.

If we are going to move to the sub-atomic level of prescribing for both equitable distributions of affective and cognitive variables within the collectivity of our office holders as well as what we hope are cognitively balanced political structures, we must have a good sense of the differences between the objective and the subjective spectra. Only this integrative understanding ensures that the entire subjective spectrum is politically represented. It will not happen by itself.

Chapter Five

Dialectics: Ideal and Material

Along with the movement to a sub-atomic understanding, and the movement to find an equitable balance across the subjective as well as the objective spectrum, a second element must be part of a cognitively based political theory. It deals with the method of history, or the dialectic, and, more specifically, it deals with the role of the two cognitions, the analytic and the synthetic, within the dialectic. The term dialectic signifies nothing more than the way history moves. It is how history gets from Stage A to Stage B, the dialectic having been central to the intellectual pantheon since the time of Zeno and Plato.

What frightens many Americans about the term dialectic is that they have more than likely heard it within the context of Karl Marx's Dialectical Materialism. The fact is that Marx's dialectic was very different from the Classical Dialectic, or the Idealist Dialectic, as it is generally referred to. What I argue is that the path to a sub-atomic, subjectively balanced political theory necessitates a return to that pre-Marxist, Idealist Dialectic, since the Materialist Dialectic, except for a few notions like false consciousness and vaguely psychological alienations, does not deal with the human mind, much less the differences among human minds.

What, then, do we mean by the Classical, or Idealist, Dialectic as opposed to the Marxist, or Materialist Dialectic? As above, one of the principal distinctions within all philosophy is the mind-object distinction. Yes, the real world surely exists, and just as surely impacts all of us, just as we impact it. But each of us also perceives and acts upon that real world just as our minds are surely impacted.

Throughout the history of philosophy, writers have argued over the relative importance of the mind and the object, just as they have speculated over how the mind and the object interact. The position that the mind leads history, the Idealist view, was the standard dialectical view from the time of the Greeks until the writings of a German philosopher named Ludwig von Feuerbach, who upended the Idealist Dialectic in 1837. The Idealist dialectical position had reigned through the death of G. W. F. Hegel in 1831 in the European cholera epidemic, and for a few years beyond under the influence of the Young Hegelians. It was still the dominant position, of course, in the time of Immanuel Kant, who died in 1804.

Had Feuerbach been the only writer to challenge the mind-first dialectic, we most likely would not pay much attention to it today. Very possibly, the reversal of the mind-object dichotomy's ordering may have been re-reversed shortly thereafter. But that was not to be, and it was not to be because of the almost immediate adoption of the Materialist Dialectic by the towering intellectual figure Karl Marx. Marx's principal political and economic writings are largely based upon, at the same time that they greatly reinforced, the Dialectical Materialism of Feuerbach, Marx arguing that we needed to "stand Hegel on his feet" when he reversed the original mind-object order. To be sure, a general intellectual positivism and the industrial age itself further ensured the dominance of Materialism.

Again, I do not believe it is possible to develop a sub-atomic, psychologically and specifically cognitively based theory of politics until we return to an Idealistic, or mind-first dialectic. No, we do not wish to return to what some call a vulgar Idealism, or the view that only the mind matters, a position that some improperly accused Hegel of holding. Similarly, vulgar interpretations of Marxism had Marx believing solely in the material world, without regard to the mind (again without much reference to psychology) that is interpretive, or historically generative. Marx in fact not only believed deeply in the world of the mind, but he retained a life-long admiration for the one whom all Europe still calls "the Philosopher" — Hegel.

And yet, it is still only the Dialectically Idealist position that places the mind first in the progress of history. If we wish to create a sub-atomic theory that brings about a more just standard of political equity by having a fair representation of subjectivities within the objectivities of political structures and processes, and if we wish to move the United States past the contradictions of a new and different century in which the American star has faded as our debts rise, our currency falls, our trade imbalances linger, and our world image fades, we need first to consider how different kinds of minds impact the dialectic. This I will attempt to do in the next chapter.

References

Friedrich Engels, "Ludwig Feuerbach and the End of Classical German Philosophy," in *Marx and Engels—Basic Writings on Politics and Philosophy,* Lewis S. Fever, ed. Garden City, Anchor Books, 1959.

Chapter Six

The Form of the Dialectic

Both Immanuel Kant and G. W. F. Hegel, with their very different preferences for cognitions, had clear if differing notions of what the dialectic contained. Kant, the more skeptical of the two as I mentioned in Chapter Two, was far more reticent concerning the ability of humankind, consciously, to advance the human condition. For Kant, the dialectic was a way of classifying knowledge, since the dialectic was more related to the Categorical, or what Kant felt was the proper placement of knowledge in various settings. History itself for Kant was largely the handiwork of Providence, not the raising of human consciousness. It was God, not the exalted pretensions of metaphysical reasoning that Kant pilloried in *The Critique of Pure Reason* and *The Prolegomena to Any Future Metaphysics Pretending to Be a Science*, which would provide for whatever progress the human condition enjoyed.

For Hegel, in contrast, the dialectic was capable of advancing the human condition; in fact that was what the dialectic was all about. Hegel's dialectic portrayed an ever-ascending level of human consciousness, with the promise of an ever-improving real world circumstance to follow. In contrast to Kant, Hegel was not only more optimistic about the dialectic; he also more closely linked the dialectic to the forms of knowledge, or the analytic and the synthetic forms that we have reviewed. Recall that Hegel considered the synthetic, or apples and oranges, form of knowledge to be superior to the analytic, apples to apples, form. In his "Idea of Cognition" chapter in *The Science of Logic*, he argued that the synthetic cognition, the cognition that Hegel argued represented a true "difference," is what enabled the dialectic to advance the human mind from one historical stage to the next.

What Hegel meant by his use of the term "difference" was a distinction in form, a qualitative not a quantitative difference, or a contrast between, say, an apple and an orange, or a can of Coke and a bottle of Coke rather than a can of Coke and a can of Pepsi. The movement through the contradictions of such different qualities was what propelled the leap to the next historical stage, the difference being part of the contradiction, at the point in history when the new understanding confronts the old.

But, and this is crucial to a new political theory, the late and highly regarded Harvard theorist Judith Shklar correctly pointed out that Hegel saw each dialectical leap of history as what she labeled a "a single, ordered whole." Oh, Hegel understood that there were three stages to the dialectic. There was the "in itself" stage, the period before the contradiction where the object is known only in its own terms, the "for itself," or contradiction stage, where the form of the old understanding is challenged by the form of the new understanding, and, finally, the "in and for itself" stage, where there is reconciliation, or rationalization, between the old and new understandings, all occurring within the novel framework that subsumes the old. Somehow, again as Professor Shklar properly understood it, Hegel's favor for the synthetic cognition led him to argue that the entire dialectical process was cognitively synthetic. He did not cognitively differentiate, in other words, between the three separate dialectical stages. But remember that Hegel was, after all, of a pre-psychological era. We, now, are privileged to borrow the psychological insights of Jung and others in the context of Bohr's sub-atomic physics. We can, indeed we must, delineate the separate cognitive character of the three dialectical stages.

So what are the cognitive qualities of the dialectic's three stages? Contrary to Hegel's "single, ordered, whole," the dialectic in fact evidences the alternation of the two grand cognitions within it. The "in itself," or first dialectical stage after all, shows the analytic form in that early historical stage when the unchallenged framework of understanding is defined only in its own terms. The "for itself," or second stage in contrast, represents the synthetic form. This, again, is where the contradiction lies, where the orange confronts the apple. The old model of understanding is being challenged by the new model of understanding, the contradiction again being in the form of those understandings, not in their substance. Then, in the "in and for itself," or third stage, the cognitive form of the dialectic returns to the analytic form. In this stage there is a rationalization, or a melding, that evidences a more robust way of understanding. Much of the old may well remain in this new, more powerful level of human consciousness, but it is fully integrated into an entirely original intellectual framework. The essential truths of justice, equity, and democracy, for example, are universal, although different historical periods dress them up in different clothes.

As optimistic as Hegel was about the human capacity for reason, as well as about the possibility for the improvement of human consciousness through history, he did not see that the cycles of history, and the dialectical progress of history, were periods in which different cognitions reigned at different dialectical periods. To bring the above understanding of the alternating cognitive nature within the dialectic to an interpretation of the structures and processes of the American government, let us look hard to see if the American political system is capable of dialectical progress. To gauge whether America's structures and processes are capable of providing for a) an equitable public policy for its own citizens and b) a successful adaptation to the political demands of a rapidly integrating world, let us now use the most well known and highly regarded of all political structure models. Let us turn to Aristotle's classical trichotomy of political structures to see if America's political system does or does not measure up.

References

Aristotle, *The Politics,* Carnes Lord, ed., Chicago, University of Chicago Press, 1984.

Judith Shklar, *Freedom and Independence: A Study of the Political Ideas of Hegel's Phenomenology of Mind,* Cambridge, Cambridge University Press, 1976.

Chapter Seven

The Aristotelian Inversion

To begin, let us define the three governmental forms of Aristotle's *Politics* within the context of a psychological theory of politics. Rule by the one, rule by the few, and rule by the many, along with the modern constitutional and sub-constitutional adaptations of that triad by far-sighted political figures like the American founders, continues after twenty-five hundred years to be the political gold standard of structural definition. Aristotle's structural trichotomy must certainly be a part of a psychologically based theory.

If the trichotomy of the one, the few, and the many is placed along a spectrum that represents only the number of people involved in a political system, as Aristotle suggested, the spectrum will merely reflect the objective variable of political circumstance, and nothing related to the mind. However, if the trichotomy is placed on a subjective, specifically cognitive spectrum, it will reflect a different configuration of structures. Recall how the objectively-based ideological spectrum bent back upon itself to reflect the same extreme on the subjective spectrum for both the objective political left and the objective political right. A similar thing happens when we insert the element of cognitions into Aristotle's three structural types. Aristotle's spectrum (based solely on the number of rulers — one, few, or many) coincides with what seems to be an appropriate cognition on only one end of the spectrum, but not on the other.

Specifically, rule by the one represents either a monarchy in a healthy political system or a tyranny in an unhealthy system. Both possess a highly synthetic cognitive form, the decisional processes of the monarchy or tyranny being highly concentrated, as we discussed earlier. Towards the center of the original Aristotelian, numerically-based spectrum, rule by the few would at first appear to involve moderately centralized institutions. One would think that the balance of centralizing to decentralizing forces within such institutions should be roughly equal. Similarly, as you move towards the other pole of the spectrum, rule by the many would at first merely involve a large number of people and might lead one to conclude that it would import the most decentralized structural arrangement. I suggest that this conclusion is incorrect, from a cognitive, sub-atomic, perspective.

What I suggest is that at the sub-atomic level, in the context of a cognitive standard of political equity, the latter two Aristotelian conditions, aristocracy and constitutional democracy, reverse. Put another way, the aristocracy of the few in a healthy system and the oligarchy of the few in an unhealthy system, are less centralized, or more decentralized, than the constitutional democracy or republic of a healthy system, or a pure democracy in an unhealthy system. That's right; the cognitive, sub-atomic, ordering of Aristotle's spectrum places an equitable, well functioning political system, a constitutional democracy or republic with its balance of analytic and synthetic cognitions, at the center of the spectrum. Aristocracy, or oligarchy, endures a cognitive imbalance in favor of the analytic cognition, at the structural pole opposite from monarchy or tyranny. It is noteworthy that Aristotle's differentiation between aristocracy and its corruption is the difference between "the distribution of prerogatives on the basis of virtue" in the case of aristocracy and that of "wealth" in the case of oligarchy. It is precisely the use of money in political ways that this philosopher, twenty-five hundred years ago, described and abhorred.

Once more, there is, or at least there should be, a balance of the private and public sectors, along with a balance of the analytic and the synthetic cognitions, at the mid-point of the spectrum. The claims of the general public and the claims on government of private interest groups are reasonably well balanced in the middle of the spectrum. Said differently, the relative weighting of analytic and synthetic cognitions at the middle of the structural spectrum reflects an equity between a relatively unencumbered contractual form

of engagement with the government, such as that used by powerful groups like the corporations, with the publicly aggregated, non-
contractual, claims of a general polity that is guaranteed a sufficient
degree of collective access to public institutions like legislatures,
administrative agencies, and at least one political party. This configuration is constitutionally democratic.

Equitable balances in public policy do not occur within an aristocracy, or its corruption, oligarchy, where the political inputs of
a few powerful individuals or interests dominate the political agenda.
Oligarchy, or rule by the few, is in fact the most decentralized form
of government; it is the form that most readily facilitates exclusive,
money-facilitated access to isolated positions of governmental decision-making by powerful interest groups. What, after all, is an
oligarchy? It is not just rule by the few, numerically, but it is rule
by the few through a *form* of access that is, again, very close to a contract, specifically an unencumbered contract, or a contract that is
able to separate itself from what might be the legitimate encumbrances of other, less powerful citizens. The dispersion of this form
of access, interestingly, comes preciously close to an all out anar-
chy, one dominated by a corrupt set of moneyed elitists in a modern polity like ours.

There are, of course, many manifestations of the above Aristotelian inversion and its balance of both sectors and analytic-to-
synthetic cognitions. I will dwell on but two of these manifestations
here. The first deals with the relationship of structure to product
or, perhaps better, of political process to political result. Just as the
undemocratic *centralization* of political power rests at one end of
Aristotle's spectrum, and at one extreme of human cruelty in the
tyrannous regimes of figures like Hitler, Stalin, and the like, something that I call *Undemocratic Decentralization* exists at the other,
oligarchic, end of the spectrum, both theoretically, and in the American political reality. The sheer number of K Street lobbyists, 40,000,
representing powerful interests that interact with the dispersed institutions of the American government, is emblematic of an oligarchic political structure.

No, the American government is not yet at the extreme of an
undemocratically decentralized government, but it is moving there.

The dispersions of government that rested in the original constitutional arrangement, with its separation of powers, federalism, its staggering of elections, its bicameralism, and its forbidding of congressional, that is legislative, members to serve in the executive branch, was followed by the nineteenth century cries of the Western and Southern populists for innovations like party primaries, and further structurally dispersing devices like the initiative, referendum, and recall. Finally, misguided academic attacks on the ostensible over-centralization of the government in books like C. Wright Mills' *The Power Elite*, followed by calls for "participatory democracy" from Tom Hayden and others of the 1960s' New Left, along with the legislative dispersion of congressional authority into committees and subcommittees that was initiated by the New Left-inspired, Democratic Party's congressional "Class of 1974," all contributed to heightened interest group vulnerability.

Please do not misunderstand. I applaud the efforts of those who champion notions like "think globally and locally." For matters like the ground water beneath our feet, the air we breathe, and the flavor of a neighborhood of homes and local stores, local action is without question the appropriate level of political response. In our personal business, the patronizing of local banks, who in turn loan to home buyers and small businesses within the community, and the choice of local stores over Big Box retailers, is laudable indeed. But, sadly, the structures of the American national government have become the best examples of how decentralization can go too far. The American government's structural decentralization has weakened the public sector in its necessary confrontation with the private sector. It has permitted the worst kind of private access to government by the few, and thwarted the public will.

Of course, there are tensions between centralizing and decentralizing forces in all organizations, from neighborhood groups to The United Nations. But the separated national institutions and the federalism that marked the original American constitutional order are now accompanied by a host of sub-constitutional devices that make the democratic aggregation of the public more difficult now than at any time since the welcome small "d" democratic reforms (such as the expansion of the franchise) that were inspired in the 1830s by Andrew Jackson. I hardly ask for some radical re-centralization of America's political institutions. Again, a moderate decentralization has its place in political systems that properly guard against abuses of concentrated powers. But undemocratic decentralization can, and I believe in our nation's case, does exist. It presages Aristotle's oligarchic political form, and movement back from that weak configuration of public structures and process, even movement ever so slightly towards the democratic world's parliamentary systems that far better balance their private sectors with healthy public institutions, is now in order for America.

A final point on centralization and decentralization. I would venture to say that an imbalance of centralizing to decentralizing vectors has also increasingly come into existence in the American electoral system. If a petty dictator wishes to pretend to the forms of democracy and therefore calls an election in which the opposition is permitted, say, to campaign for but one week and spend but $5,000, the election would be a sham, would it not? But what if an election were held where the campaigning had to begin immediately after the previous election and the total expenditures for the election had to reach the sum of $3,000,000,000, as occurred with the 2008 American federal elections and even more in 2012? Oh, some of that money might be called "good" money, made up of small contributions, raised personally, mostly on the internet, without contractually formed strings attached. But a great deal of money was not raised that way in the so-called reform elections of 2008 or in 2012. Much of the big money had, and continues to have, strings, and its contributors expect a contractual, oligarchic form of relationship with the victorious office holder. In short, if the dictator's $5,000 fig leaf election is perhaps best called a Type I Undemocratic Election, at one end of the spectrum, the election at the other pole might best be called a Type II Undemocratic Election.

In Part Two, I will examine what I consider to be three crucial foundations for the development of a sub-atomic, subjectively based political philosophy. First, I will argue for why we need to extend the limits to knowledge that have been found in the evolving epistemological debates that began with John Locke and continued up through G. W. F. Hegel, they dealing with the use of the analytic and synthetic cognitive forms in relation to *a priori*, or reasoned knowledge, and *a posteriori*, or evidentiary knowledge. Second, I will briefly review what I have written about in other places regarding what I believe to be the pattern of emergence of the cognitive forms as the principal epistemological divide in Western philosophy. Third, I will discuss why I believe that what have been the principal left political positions over the last years cannot assist us in getting to the position of the Psychological, or Natural Left.

References

Aristotle, *The Complete Works of Aristotle,* vol. 2. Princeton: Princeton University Press, 1984.

Part Two

Contexts and Contradictions

Chapter Eight

Beyond the Synthetic *a Priori*

As before, the heart of any political theory is its standard of fairness, or justice, accompanied by its design for a polity's approach to that standard. My quest for a new equitable standard is based on nothing more than the demand that the entire psychological spectrum, including its component affective and cognitive ranges, be a) fairly included in the contemporary political dialogue, b) fairly included in the design of the structures and processes of the government that brokers that dialogue, and c) fairly represented within the dialectic that moves the political dialogue through its necessary historical transitions.

This chapter attempts to do nothing more than parsimoniously outline the history of the limits of what could reasonably be known throughout the history of Western thought. To what extent anything can confidently be known is one of the most important of intellectual arguments. To help get a grip on this question, I will utilize the dichotomy of the analytic and synthetic cognitions as it interacts with the dichotomy of *a priori*, or reason-based, thought and *a posteriori*, or evidence-based, thought. These two dichotomies marched alongside each other in the progress of Western intellectual history. Their collateral progress, which I suggest can and should be extended one more step, permits the creation of another pillar for a cognitively balanced government.

There is a history to the development of what we can know, beginning in modern thought with the English philosopher John Locke's position that no *a priori*, or reason-based thinking, is truly knowable. The mind, for Locke, was a *tabula rasa*, all information coming from experience. Following Locke, the German mathematician Samuel von Pufendorf argued that at least some things could be known beyond what Locke permitted. Pufendorf allowed that analytic thought, the form of thought Pufendorf worked with in mathematics for example, could be known *a priori*. In other words, things of a like, or apples and apples, nature could be known by reason alone. No empirical, or evidence based knowledge, was necessary to extend the sphere of what could be known if one was only talking about analytic forms, according to Pufendorf.

After Pufendorf came Immanuel Kant, he again of the analytic mind. As we have seen with the equation $7 + 5 = 12$, Kant argued that nearly all of mathematics was synthetic, not analytic. Math, according to Kant, usually dealt with the uneven balances of numbers. Kant also believed that mathematical conclusions constituted a progress of knowledge and that mathematics, along with natural science, was knowable, *a priori*, or by reason. The skeptic in Kant, as we have reviewed, came out in his contempt for the French *philosophes* and metaphysicians generally. In form, what they claimed to know was synthetic, like math and science, and it was *a priori*, like math and science as well. But metaphysics, as we reviewed earlier, was too abstract for Kant, as well as being altogether too speculative. Further, metaphysics lacked the "intersubjectivity" that Kant required for all knowledge. To Kant, we couldn't declare something as known until everyone understood it in the same way. Metaphysics, clearly, could never claim such unanimity.

Next in this much abbreviated history of knowledge's growing limits came G. W. F. Hegel. The Philosopher, with his synthetic mind, thought speculatively. His depiction of the dialectical progress of the human mind in the *Phenomenology* relied on an ever-improving, synthetically *a priori*, set of understandings of philosophical truth that we have heretofore seen the roots of. Again, Hegel favored the synthetic over the analytic cognition, arguing that it was a more complex form of understanding and arguing as well that the *a priori* synthetic cognition, or reasoned cognition, was foundational for the dialectic. Indeed it was, although I do not believe it was exclusively so.

As above, the roles for the two grand cognitions, the analytic and the synthetic, along with the roles of the two origins of knowledge, the *a priori* and the *a posteriori*, played out in the context of expanded limits of knowledge and their correspondingly new philosophical comprehensions. In the dialectic, a framework of understanding, by definition, achieves a level of homeostasis, or equilibrium, at least for a time. That equilibrium, once again, imports a dominance of the analytic cognition. Then, in the way in which the old structure of knowing things is challenged by a new structure of knowing things, the new variables are challenged, again in a synthetic, or apples to oranges, way.

I believe there is one more historical stage beyond Hegel's synthetic *a priori*. It is the stage in which the analytic and the synthetic cognition, and their relative perspectives on things, are known simultaneously. What I suggest is that achieving an equity of knowledge forms, by simultaneously utilizing both forms, is the condition precedent for political fairness, and legal equity. Just as the dialectic is not of a "single, ordered whole," containing but one cognition (Hegel's favorite synthetic cognition), and just as the dialectic in fact includes the alternating impact of the analytic and the synthetic cognitions respectively, so too the everyday operation of any government's structures and processes must reflect equity, and balance, between the two cognitions in order to guarantee both subatomic political equity. Over time, again, the two cognitions must remain simultaneously available.

What the extension of the limits to knowledge beyond Hegel's preference for the synthetic *a priori* can bring about is what I see as a grand cognitive bargain. The inclusion of the synthetic cognition equally with the analytic cognition, within the context of the limits of knowledge as described above, must be accompanied by the inclusion of the synthetic cognition in the structural, that is constitutional, arrangements that underlie American politics as well as in the consideration of specific political issues. Knowing things simultaneously in different ways, and arriving at just political solutions, are clearly linked. If the Natural Left is to insist upon equal status for synthetically formed thought, all the while rejecting Hegel's claim for the superiority of the synthetic over the analytic cognition in the context of the limits to knowledge, then the American political system, in order to ensure equitable results, must consciously reject its implicit claim for the superiority of the analytic cognition. That is the grand bargain concerning the analytic and the synthetic cognitive forms, moving one step beyond Hegel's historical stage of the synthetic *a priori* to the equal incorporation of both cognitions, and their political progeny.

References

John Locke, *An Essay Concerning Human Understanding*, New York, Dover, 1959.

Samuel von Pufendorf, *On The Duty of Man and Citizen According to Natural Law*, Cambridge, Cambridge Texts in the History of Political Thought, 1991.

Chapter Nine

Cognition in Intellectual History

All theory needs ballast, and that ballast must come from somewhere. Maybe the longer the intellectual bloodline, the greater the credibility of the claim for ballast will be. In this chapter, I will summarize something I worked with many years ago. It was an intellectual history, one that depicted the rise of the analytic-to-synthetic cognitive differentiation to a position of epistemological dominance in Western thought. I am not an intellectual historian. What I did was sketchy and, I'm sure, suffered gaps. Nonetheless, I do believe I offered at least a measure of evidence for the existence of a pattern in Western intellectual history that revealed the emerging importance of the cognitive variable in so many discussions over the nature of knowledge itself. The study of knowledge, and its various schools, must include the study of the forms of knowledge and how those forms relate to the method, and ultimately the substance, of various intellectual, and political, positions.

For the Greeks, there were two principal intellectual schools: the rational and the skeptical. The rationalists, sometimes more and sometimes less, believed two things. They believed, first, that there was an order to the world and, second, that humankind could at least reasonably well divine that order. The skeptics, in contrast, believed one of two things. First, many believed that there was no order to the world. The world was simply a random place. Alternatively, some skeptics admitted that though there may be an order to the world, that order was too obscure, too unapproachable, for humankind to understand it. Hence their skepticism.

Now let me suggest how the cognitive variable intruded on, but also guided, all of this. With the rational school, what I submit is that there was an important difference between the cognitive forms of someone like Plato's description of the political world (at least in *The Republic*) and those of Aristotle. Plato's ideal state included the philosopher king, the guardians, and a variety of other ranked orders down through the slaves. In form, the key element of the Platonic vision was organic, built upon the interaction that existed among differentiated orders. It all fit, according to Plato, and it fit because each status played its separate but indispensable role.

The Aristotelian political order was not at all like the Platonic order. With Aristotle, almost any Greek citizen might hold a position of leadership. It was best, in fact, if political leadership rotated. For Aristotle, other roles were also interchangeable within the larger political society. The system, in short, tended towards the mechanistic over the organic, and the interchangeable roles imported a far greater similarity of citizen attributes within the polity. Aristotle's largely, of course not wholly, analytic vision is correctly viewed as being amenable to a more small "d" democratic vision than Plato's largely synthetic vision. More citizens could be envisioned in places of leadership.

Once again, our attention should be directed to the cognitive forms, as they are linked to the skeptical/rational divide. The organic form, with all of its parts being highly differentiated, is far more synthetic than analytic. The mechanistic form is more analytic with, again, its parts being more interchangeable because they are more similar. With regard to Western intellectual history, I suggest that this cognitive distinction became very important. To see this, let us look first at the cognitive nature, or natures, of the classically skeptical intellectual position.

As with the rationalists, there were two cognitively differentiated ways to be skeptical. Wholly apart from the don't-know-or-can't-tell dichotomy mentioned earlier, there were two distinctly different cognitive forms available within the skeptical position. The first grew out of the position that something can be known but cannot be known with *exactitude*, that being because the perceiver was involved in the knowing, and all perceivers are not alike.

They lack, as above, what Kant would call "intersubjectivity." The above is essentially the "soft," or relativistic, response to the rationalists, as evidenced in the "man is the measure of all things" position of Protagoras, or in Heraclitus's reflections on flux, or perpetual change.

The alternative, or what may fairly be called the "hard" relativistic position, is perhaps best evidenced by Thrasymachus, who argued that there was no rational order to the political world because in the final analysis the single element of power dictated all political relations. The strong invariably won out over the weak, regardless of how any natural, or created, political order might have attempted to justly mete out the rewards of political existence at one time.

In sum, what we take away from the Greeks is something quite simple, once the cognitive forms of the two sub-positions (as they existed within the two grand rational and skeptical philosophical perspectives) are understood. Each of the two grand positions possessed a cognitively analytic, and a cognitively synthetic, sub-category. As you might have predicted, those two sub-schools slowly fell away from each other, leading to a realignment of the epistemological range. That range, by the late eighteenth and early nineteenth century times of Kant and Hegel respectively, wound up reflecting the cognitive preferences of these Idealist figures rather than the original, rational versus skeptical, cognitively bicameral, range. Unlikes separated themselves from each other. Then, likes, over a good deal of time to be sure, attracted each other and the cognitive distinction grew to supersede the pre-sub-atomic non-cognitive distinction.

Kant's intellectual roots resided only in part, therefore, with the rationalists. As we have said, his penchant for precision scorned the French *philosophes.* He preferred the "common sense" notions of a philosopher like Jean Jacques Rousseau, who rejected the more grandiose of French philosophical claims. From the skeptical side, Kant followed Hume's laudable separation of the mind and object, even though Hume could not decide which element came first. In what Kant called his answer to Hume's question, the German philosopher placed the mind ahead of the object, thus completing the line of anti-philosophical empiricism that had begun with Locke by implanting it firmly within German Idealism. This, of course, was compatible with Königsberg's best analytic mind, and it is well known as the Copernican Revolution in philosophy. For Hegel, the cognitively generated story is structurally similar, if substantively very different. From the skeptical side of the rational-to-skeptical continuum, Hegel borrowed from Montesquieu, one of his few predecessors for whom he had much intellectual respect. Montesquieu's understanding of cultural relativity underlay his justifications for a relativity in the law that could be found in different societies, rejecting Cicero's classical notion of one law, universal, for all time and all people. If you see a bit of Protagoras in Montesquieu, and Hegel, you are right.

From the rational side, it is important to remember that Hegel never fully outgrew the religious training he received at the Tübingen Seminary just outside his native Stuttgart. Hegel's early writings on the humanistic Jesus incorporated a strong moral sense, and though the allure of the Enlightenment was surely dimmed following the Terror, Hegel nonetheless continued to embrace Enlightenment perspectives on nature and the progress of history, all placed comfortably within that ascendance of human consciousness that is the core of the *Phenomenology*. Hegel, after all, rooted for Napoleon at the 1806 Battle of Jena, the joust that served as the *coup de grace* for the Holy Roman Empire. Of course his preference in that battle also served as the *coup de grace* for Hegel's teaching career in Jena.

In short, the grand pattern of cognitive intrusion into the original rational/skeptical divide is one of fission-fusion. If I had asked a physicist about all of this at the outset, I suspect I would have been more confident about what I was finding. The epistemological fission-fusion describes an original, cognitively-based separation, and subsequent reconfiguration, of the twin intellectual alliances that eventually converged along the cognitively compatible lines described above. It began with the Greek divide, and, perhaps not surprisingly, Immanuel Kant and G. W. F. Hegel wound up being the best modern exemplars of the analytic and the synthetic cognitive preference. But, just as importantly, their very different notions of Dialectical Idealism marked what I believe were the two confluence points of the analytic and synthetic positions in Western intellectual history.

As one might anticipate, similar fission-fusion patterns have occurred in other intellectual arenas. I will detail but one here. In the theory of law, or jurisprudence, the fission-fusion pattern reveals the gathering dominance of the cognitive dimension over the two original, non-cognitive jurisprudential schools of natural law and positive law, they themselves being derivative of the rationalist and skeptical philosophical positions respectively. On the natural law side, the legal writings of Plato and Aristotle are instructive for Cicero, Seneca, and even the Byzantine Emperor Justinian into the sixth century whose *Corpus Juris* was so important for the development of European Civil Law.

Moving out of the middle ages, the divide within the natural law position begins with the writings of the Englishman Richard Hooker, who hung on to the human collectivity with one hand while with the other he began a modern discussion of rights that led to the individualistic sense of rights that flowered under John Locke. Thus, though Locke's notions were substantively influenced by his more collectivist predecessor Hooker, they were methodologically influenced by the mathematician that we've already introduced, Samuel von Pufendorf. Pufendorf had a great influence on Voltaire and on those legal thinkers we've already cited in France known as the "legislationists." The dual pretensions of certainty and precision within this school were a large part of what rankled Kant, as earlier, although the same addiction to certainty and precision marked Sir William Blackstone's *Commentaries* in England.

Blackstone, who railed against a post-Glorious Revolution parliamentary statute book that had "swelled to ten times a larger bulk," was greatly influenced by the English philosopher Thomas Hobbes. Hobbes, though of the Imperative, or positive law school substantively, insisted on a level of methodological precision and predictability that Blackstone mimicked in his volumes on English legal history and jurisprudence. With Voltaire and Blackstone, as well as with Kant who once insisted that "completeness" was his "chief aim" in the law, the analytic cognitive tilt is readily apparent. Not incidentally, Jeremy Bentham, much the positivist, was harshly critical of Blackstone and his natural law groundings while his own jurisprudential writings strongly reflected the same quest for precision and self-equilibration that Blackstone's writings revealed. It was the *origins* of Blackstone's position alone that Bentham found so repellent. Its method, and its cognitive biases, were both much closer to Bentham than the nineteenth century utilitarian may have wanted to admit.

On the cognitively synthetic side of the ledger, the fission and fusion pattern is similar, if somewhat more complex and longer running before the cognitive confluence of the prior synthetic natural and positive law positions is achieved. The "softer" edges of the Romans Cicero and Seneca, as above, along with the Byzantine Justinian, are reflected centuries later in different nations' attempts to give a vitality, and regeneration, to the law. For the Germans, it was the historicists, Frederick von Savigny, G.F. Puchta, and, into the twentieth century, Rudolf Stammler, who maintained an evolutionary vision of the law, the rarely modest Hegel being too critical of Savigny's provincialism in my judgment. For the French, the birth of the Sociological School in France grew largely from the broadly gauged legal writings of Léon Duguit, while in the United States Roscoe Pound argued for a similarly purposive law that took into account the current condition of the citizenry as part of that citizenry's legitimate demands for redress. Though surely not of the Sociological School, even Oliver Wendell Holmes, Jr.'s *Common Law* argued for the primacy of experience over logic, that measure of experience generously including considerations that in the first instance were not legal, and certainly richer than the sterile calculus of precedent and mechanistic interpretation that typified traditional common law methodology.

The rather dramatic confluence of the natural and positive law positions on the cognitively synthetic side, I suggest, occurred all within one volume, the 1958 *Harvard Law Review*. It was there that the Oxford Chair of Jurisprudence, H. L. A. Hart, who had dueled in his native England with legal conservatives like Lord Patrick Devlin over matters such as the outlawing of homosexuality and who was in many ways a descendant of Hans Kelsen whose concept of the "pure theory" of law included a rich mixture of flexible contexts for finding the law, argued the positivist position in contradistinction to the Harvard Law School's Chair of Jurisprudence Lon Fuller's argument for natural law.

Of course, the *Harvard Law Review* represented these writings as the champion-like thrustings of the two grand jurisprudential schools. I don't think that was what was going on. At the sub-atomic, or the cognitive level, these writings marked the confluence of the synthetic jurisprudential position, the product of a jurisprudential rearrangement that led to the sub-atomic configuration. Hart argued on the positivist side of the jurisprudential ledger within the framework of what he labeled the "primary" considerations in the law, these representing deep patterns of social and political custom, all taking their place at the point of contact between law and such externalities. Secondary considerations, or what Hart saw principally as matters of a barren legal procedure, did not contain such fullness of content, Hart's distinction between the levels of the law being not far away from the notion that law's legitimacy implies a descent from something higher, and broader, even if it is custom in the first instance and not morality.

At Harvard, Lon Fuller had become the heroic figure that he was in Western jurisprudence because of his revival of the natural law in the twentieth century, his perspective being out of jurisprudential fashion for nearly one hundred and fifty years, or since the Revolution. The natural law was supplanted by far less philosophically grounded notions of law throughout the entire nineteenth century, a supplanting that was fortified by the artistic romanticism, political nationalism, and economic industrialism that blanketed the century. As earlier, positivism ruled.

In short, the positions of Hart and Fuller were nowhere near as cognitively, or even substantively, apart as their Harvard pieces at first appeared to represent when one looks at their very similar favor for a mosaic in the law, a content that included morality, custom, and culture within it, as well as a historical progression of the law in keeping with the times. Perhaps most of all, both of these gentlemen possessed a keen sense of what a just law, or a law with *ius* being superior to *lex*, should provide for its citizenry. Rather than

the natural law and the positive law being paraded in their traditional vestments in Harvard's journal, therefore, the 1958 Hart and
Fuller articles, I believe, represented the ascendancy of the sub-
atomic continuum over the pre-sub-atomic continuum. Each position represented, once more, a robust half of the cognitively
synthetic fusion in Western jurisprudence. In a rough sort of way,
I think that this jurisprudential confluence, in concert with the
confluence of Bentham's and Blackstone's cognitively sympathetic
fusion on the cognitively analytic side, represents something very
much like the philosophical fission and fusion that I described with
Kant and Hegel.

Beyond the law and jurisprudence, a far more short-term, cognitively relevant pattern blossomed in Western economic theory,
the resultant divide being illustrated by the differences between the
so-called Chicago School, with its micro economics-oriented, price
theory mechanics (so much of which was the product of the Nobel
prize winning Milton Friedman's "I don't understand what an ex-
ternality is" and those others who believed in a self-corrective and
spontaneously equitable market) as opposed to John Maynard
Keynes' and the earlier Alfred Marshall notions of macro economics, with their correspondingly less sanguine view of how individual economic activity necessarily provided for grander equilibriums.
Methodologically, this latter position had its roots in the more self-
consciously interdisciplinary writings of political economists like
David Ricardo, John Stuart Mill, or even Adam Smith in his early
writings on morality.

To be sure, the cognitively synthetic position clearly imported
something beyond Adam Smith's "invisible hand" and resulted in
the regulatory, fiscal, and monetary involvement of government in
the economy. After all, even Adam Smith had candidly acknowledged
the tendency of manufacturers to "combine" and fix prices, as well
as the ability of manufacturers to hold out longer than workers in
labor disputes. The product of that government involvement, I
submit, is almost invariably synthetic, the public encumbrance on
a private contract balancing the analytic form with cognitively dissimilar considerations.

I am delighted, incidentally, by the recent insights of writers like Dan Ariely on what is most frequently called "behavioral economics." Ariely properly dismisses the pretensions of those who believed in the "rational" behavior of individuals and then underpinned so much of traditional economics on such assumptions. Lately, this nonsense has been thoroughly undermined by evidence revealing the non-rational, psychologically dictated conduct of individuals in real world economic settings. In a dramatic *volte-face*, the Booth School of business at the University of Chicago recently advertised in the *Tribune* that it has eight psychologists on their faculty. It's about time. The almost exclusive use of the analytic cognition, at the highest levels of twentieth century orthodox economic theory, is finally getting its comeuppance. A belief in the purest forms of capitalism has never been anything more than a surrender to the exclusive use of the analytic cognition by those who didn't wish to, or couldn't, use the other side of their brain. There are some signs that we are now growing out of all of that. To help do this, let us next examine the three major reasons for why we have not yet arrived at the sub-atomic level of theory in politics.

References

Dan Ariely, *Predictably Irrational: The Hidden Forces That Shape Our Decisions*, New York, Harper, 2008.

Jeremy Bentham, *The Theory of Legislation,* New York, Harcourt Brace, 1931.

William Blackstone, *Commentaries,* New York, Augustus M. Kelly, 1969.

Lon Fuller, "Positivism and Fidelity to Law — A Reply to Professor Hart", *Harvard law Review*, Vol. 71, Feb. 1958.

Milton Friedman, *Capitalism and Freedom,* Chicago, University of Chicago Press, 1962.

H. L. A. Hart, "Positivism and the Separation of Law and Morals," *Harvard Law Review, Vol.* 71, Feb. 1958.

Thomas Hobbes, *Leviathan,* ed. By John Charles Gaskin, Oxford, Oxford University Press, 1988.

Oliver Wendell Holmes, Jr., *The Common Law,* New York, Little Brown, 1909.

Richard Hooker, "The Doctrine of Natural Law," in Robert Lindsay Schoettinger, ed. *The Conservative Tradition in European Thought,* New York, Putnam's, 1970.

John Maynard Keynes, *"The General Theory of Employment, Interest, and Money,* New York, Harcourt Brace, 1935.

Hans Kelsen, *The Pure Theory of Law,* trans. By Charles H. Wilson, *Law Quarterly Review,* vol. 71, 1958.

William P. Kreml, *Relativism and the Natural Left,* New York, New York University Press, 1984

John Locke, "Essays on the Law of Nature," in Paul E. Sigmund, ed. *Natural Law in Political Thought,* Cambridge, Winthrop, 1971.

Alfred Marshall, see Eric Roll, *A History of Economic Thought,* London, Faber and Faber, 1956.

Baron de Montesquieu, "The Spirit of the Laws," in Melvin Richter, ed. *The Political Theory of Montesquieu,* Cambridge, Cambridge University Press, 1977.

Roscoe Pound, "A Theory of Social Interests," Papers of the American Sociological Society, vol. 15, 1921.

G. F. Puchta, *Outlines of The Science of Jurisprudence: An Introduction To The Systematic Study of Law,* Edinburgh, T. & T. Clark, 1887.

Frederick von Savigny, *On The Vocations Of Our Age For Legislation and Jurisprudence,* trans. by Abraham Hayward, London, Littlewood and Co, 1831.

Adam Smith, *An Inquiry Into The Nature and Causes of The Wealth of Nations,* New York, Modern Library, 1937.

Rudolf Stammler, "Fundamental Tendencies in Modern Jurisprudence," *Michigan law Review, Vol. 21,* 1923.

Voltaire, Jean Francois Marie Arouet, Quoted in Paul Edwards, ed. *The Encyclopedia of Philosophy,* New York, MacMillan and the Free Press, 1967.

Chapter Ten

The False Prophets

Socialism and the Co-ops

In this final chapter of Part Two, I will broach a consideration that I hope will further deepen the intellectual foundation of a psychologically grounded political philosophy. I believe this consideration to be indispensable to our theory because it should enhance our comprehension of why the cross weave of subjective considerations with the just claims of objectively based groups must become a part of the political left.

To begin, please recall my double-lined, objective and subjective spectrum model in Chapter Four. The objective spectrum, as you remember, curls back to the right in its last rush to something comparable to the Stalinist left which, as we discussed, is representative of the subjective, or psychological, right. There were many brands of socialism, communism being the most extreme of course. But even with communism, Lenin, the most successful of communists as we referenced before, cautioned against ruinous extremism. As we reviewed in the above discussion of the objective and subjective continua, there is a break point in the objectively-based ideological spectrum. The early utopian socialisms, often underpinned by an unconscious but clearly psychologically left of center religious orientation such as that of the early Christians, were near that break point, near the home of the Natural Left.

Within the American experience, the democratic socialist tradition, which was embraced by such figures as Eugene Debs and Norman Thomas, for example, borrowed its platform from European sources like the German Social Democratic Party. German theorists and activists such as Wilhelm Liebknecht were not totalitarian in their politics, and their descendants in the United States were not either. In the rare instances when American socialists achieved electoral success, they usually proved to be anything but arbitrary in their rule. Milwaukee, Wisconsin had socialist mayors in thirty-eight of the fifty years between 1910 and 1960, with Frank P. Zeidler, the last significant Socialist office holder in this country until the coming of Vermont's now Senator Bernie Sanders, governing Milwaukee from 1948 to 1960 with a deeply humanistic perspective. Zeidler artfully combined his religious Lutheranism with a *Mittel European* balance of individual and collective claims on the polity. He understood the distinction between the *gemeinschaft* and the *gesellschaft*, and the meaning of the *gemütlichkeit*, the calm of being part of a nurturant community. Victor Berger, also a socialist, served in the Congress during portions of the second and third decades of the twentieth century, representing Milwaukee. A young Milwaukee school teacher named Golda Mabovitch lived in the Zionist socialist tradition and, long after marrying a man named Meir, became the prime minister of Israel.

I remember well the warm conversation I had with the late Mayor Zeidler many years ago. Also, I do not forget that it was the German Social Democrats who courageously decided to come to the Reichstag and vote "no" after Chancellor Paul von Hindenburg's 1933 disastrous appointment of Adolf Hitler to the German presidency. The party continued leafleting in the streets until August of 1934, its members paying a heavy price for their activity.

In Illinois, figures like the near socialist, German born Democratic governor, John Peter Altgeld, who freed the remaining (some having already been executed) Haymarket Affair prisoners in Chicago and fought the gold Democrat President Grover Cleveland and his railroad lawyer Attorney General Richard Olney on the side of Eugene V. Debs and the American Railway Union during the 1894 Pullman strike, along with the great trial attorney Clarence Darrow (Altgeld's young law partner in their office on Diversey Blvd. after the governor's single term), as well as figures like the socialist women's advocate Jane Addams, were all well within the democratic tradition. They too had much of the subjective, natural, left within them.

But as we have discussed, ideologies on the left of the logical, or objective, political spectrum were not always so clearly of one psychological shade or the other. On the one hand, the Midwest application of co-op principles concerning things like factory governance, as they were practiced in companies like the Cummins Engine Company of Columbus, Indiana, were more than likely of the subjective left. The enlightened vision of a business owner like J. Irwin Miller, a liberal Christian, president of the American Council of Churches, and American representative to the World Council of Churches, was evidenced by deep worker loyalty to his company. Along with other companies—the Lincoln Electric Company of Cleveland, Ohio; Ben Heinemann's Chicago and Northwestern Railway; and Bill Patterson's United Airlines—Cummins provided for worker democracy, job rotation, and a pattern of reward that reflected true equity, all coupled with a humane environment in the work place. The conservative American columnist George Will may wish to disavow it today, but early in his journalistic career he wrote a favorable piece on the role of co-ops in worker-management relations, properly citing Midwestern examples.

But, we must remember, the notions of worker participation in the management of a workplace were not always so gentle. The syndicalist writings of those like Arthur Petersen and Daniel De Léon, for example, evidenced a hard shell notion of irremediable class contradiction, to be addressed by union ownership of industries, and were almost certainly not of the subjective left. Similarly, although the struggles of the Industrial Workers of the World has been the stuff of leftist legend, the actual conduct of many Wobblies, whether or not they acted under the influence of trenchant leaders like Big Bill Haywood, was often violent and too seldom transcendent of class divisions during the labor battles of the West and other regions.

Overseas, America's Abraham Lincoln Brigade, in its fight for the Republican government in the Spanish Civil War, sometimes in the company of volunteers from the by-then exiled German Social Democratic Party, evidenced divisions between the objective, fre-

quently Marxist, left and the softer left, just as the Spanish Popular Front itself had contained subjectively left figures who recon-
ciled and cooperated with others in the Front as opposed to the
Stalinists who marched solely to the invariably disruptive com-
mands of the Soviet.

I refer to the above examples, reviewing some contrasting, objectively based, economic and political rights positions in an incomplete manner to be sure, only to highlight further the real world
contrast between the objective spectrum and the subjective spectrum
that we reviewed earlier. Although there may have been much within
some of the socialisms, and syndicalism, that included the subjective left, neither the socialist nor syndicalist positions guaranteed
the leadership, or the equitable participation within the ranks, of
a Debs, (an Alsatian whose parents settled in Terre Haute, Indiana), a Zeidler, an Addams, or others of the natural or psychological left psychology like Cummins's Mr. Miller. Socialism and a
derivative like syndicalism were not built on the subjective distinction, and they did not always provide for it. But neither did at
least two other pre-psychological perspectives, one political and
one philosophical

The New Left

The political ideology known as The New Left blossomed in the
United States with the publishing of C. Wright Mills' *Power Elite*
in 1956. Although the principal message of that work achieved a
broad measure of acceptance, not only within the Academy but
also within President Dwight D. Eisenhower's famous admonition
concerning "the military-industrial complex" in his Farewell Address
of 1960, the structural subtext of Mills' work is also important to
understand. Throughout the book that the peace-seeking Eisenhower cited after the disappointing scrubbing of his meeting with
the Soviet leader Nikita Khrushchev (America's Frances Gary Powers U-2 spy plane having just been shot down over the Soviet
Union), Mills repeatedly referred to the excessive centralization of
the American political system. Read just the first two chapters of

the book and see how often Mills returns to that theme. The same mantra was elaborated on six years later by the student activist Thomas Hayden, whose Students for a Democratic Society's opening speech at Port Huron, Michigan hailed the notion of "participatory democracy." With participatory democracy, all citizens would be entitled, directly, to take part in each of the public decisions that impacted their lives. This was the answer to what Hayden, like Mills, saw as the excessive centralization of power in the American political system.

There are problems with the notion of participatory democracy on two levels. First, participatory democracy comes too close, theoretically, to the pure democracy that is as much a corruption of Aristotle's constitutional democracy, or republican government, as oligarchy is of aristocracy at the other end of the sub-atomic spectrum. But even more importantly, the real world manifestations of direct democracy permeated the real world office holders of the Democratic Party "Class of 1974" who infected the House of Representatives with the kinds of decentralizing stratagems in the internal arrangements of congressional committees that we have already discussed. The law of unintended consequences raised its head with a vengeance, congressional decentralization clearing the way for private sector interest groups to gain ever greater access to our government.

It wasn't until later in the nineteen-sixties, with the prescient writings of the knowledgeable political scientist Theodore Lowi, that there was a sound, theoretically grounded, response to the overly decentralist prescriptions of writers like Mills and Hayden. In his *End of Liberalism*, Lowi defined the nature of what he called "access points," whereby powerful interest groups interacted directly and favorably with either legislative or regulatory institutions within the government. Lowi then defined what he called the "captive agency," wherein the interest group came to so dominate regulatory agencies like the Food and Drug Administration and the Federal Aviation Authority that appointments to these panels were often cleared by the industry and then monitored closely for regulatory "friendliness" by those who were supposed to be monitored.

All too frequently, the appointments fell to former members of the industry itself.

Before he finished, Lowi described a grand design of mid-range theory that he called "The Iron Triangle." This political model portrayed the triad of office holder, regulatory agency or legislative entity, and the interest group as locked in a political back scratch that benefited all players, at least in the short run, to the detriment of the public good. In his descriptions of large, targeted campaign contributions, favorable regulatory rulings, and increased funding for agencies that "played ball" with the office holder by favoring contributor interest groups, Lowi responded to the decentralizing arguments of the New Left by advocating stronger political parties and meaningful public sector responses to the private corporations.

Though not from a perspective of a cognitively based theory of politics, Prof. Lowi went on to argue in the *End of Liberalism* that excessive decentralization invariably impacts who wins and who loses in the political game. The wealthier, more powerful political actor greatly benefited from the isolated situs of the governmental decision point, Lowi claimed, implicitly if not explicitly rejecting the notion of the noted liberal economist John Kenneth Galbraith, that "countervailing powers" could be counted on to balance interest groups and provide for the equitable weighting of governmental input. In a significant way, Lowi's writings assisted me in my coming to the inversion of two elements of the Aristotelian trichotomy, with the oligarchic rule by the few benefiting from the dispersion of governmental institutions to the detriment of representational, or constitutional, democracy, thus lining up on the opposite structural pole from the over-centralized monarchy or tyranny.

But beyond the excessive decentralization of the Congress specifically, and of the entire political system generally, inequities in the system would occur, Lowi claimed, because of the growing weakness of integrating public sector institutions like political parties. Lowi rejected the New Deal era claim of party advocate E. E. Schattschneider that parties could easily subsume interest groups, and thus provide for equitable government. Incidentally, members of the Democratic Party that I talk with rarely know that Professor Lowi parted the ivy and entered the world of politics in the year 2000. He served on the steering committee of the Green Party presidential candidate, Ralph Nader, knowledgeably reinforcing that candidate's soon to be realized warnings about increasing private power in the political world.

Post-Modernism

If the various brands of socialism did not provide for sub-atomic balances between the analytic and the synthetic cognition, and accordingly prescribe for equitable government within the democratic tradition, and if the New Left of the nineteen-sixties, even with its more psychological bent as expressed in Hayden's writings about a "new generation" raised in "modest comfort" did not address the biases of undemocratic decentralization, what remained to benefit the left?

Please permit an all too adumbrated discussion of a non-political philosophical perspective that had a considerable impact on American political thinking, particularly on the campuses of many universities and colleges, and most especially within the faculties and graduate student populations of the humanities and social sciences. I am referring to the perspective known as post-modernism. I am hardly an expert on post-modernism, but I believe I understand it well enough to know that this largely European philosophy did have a significant, if indirect, influence on the politics of our country. What, then, is post-modernism?

The smart aleck answer is that post-modernism comes after modernism, which is not even true, except perhaps in a field like architecture wherein the Mies van der Rohe, Second Chicago School of minimalist steel and glass, as in the Chicago River's IBM building or New York's Seagram's or Lever buildings, was followed by the Chippendale-style ornamentation of New York's A. T. & T. headquarters. The assumed completeness and unity of modernism was challenged by the new complication of the often non-functional, ornamental, addition.

But post-modernism is far more than architecture, and, rather than following modernism chronologically, it more fully stands as an intellectual response to the kind of neo-Enlightenment modernist claim of progress, inherent political fairness, and the assumed ascendance of reason as the principal engine of history. Writers like Jean-Francois Lyotard challenged these modernist notions in the 1970s, though the term post-modern had been around for nearly a century before. At its root, post-modernism did nothing less than challenge the certainty, and the universality, of meaning itself. To know things too well, or too confidently, a post-modernist might say, is to miss the contingencies, the relativities, and the nuances of all thought.

The French philosopher Jacques Derrida also spoke to the elusiveness of meaning. The very notion of definition rankled Derrida, who saw it as an attempt to capture and overly organize thought that should not be so constricted. Derrida's notions of "deconstruction" insisted on discontinuities and the lack of fit in the definitional assemblage of knowledge. For Derrida, there was no higher universal of understanding that would arbitrate, and categorize, the lesser holdings, and their contradictions.

Perhaps the most influential of all the post-modernists on American campuses was the Frenchman Michel Foucault. Foucault's writings most frequently dealt with institutions, and the rigid, stultifying nature of institutional orthodoxies. He began with an attack on the brutality of prisons, but in many ways the prison became a template for his later critiques of other modern organizations. In that way, his work mirrored Tom Hayden's writing about the dullness and morbidity of all modern bureaucracy in the latter's SDS clarion.

I apologize for the brevity of the above review as I certainly acknowledge post-modernism as a serious philosophical perspective, within the bounds of accurate understandings of its principal writings. It made a contribution. Also, it is important to say that much of the criticism of post-modernism not only came unfairly from those who did not understand it, or perhaps who found its sometimes ephemeral nature too threatening, but also from those who criticized the extensions of post-modernism that grew out of the writings of lesser philosophic and academic thinkers. It was they who sometimes extended post-modernism into a nihilistic, there-can-never-be-any-meaning kind of interpretation. The original post-modernists did not say that. Their sense of the contingency of meaning, if I may generalize about them, did import a kind of meaning. That meaning was not nihilistic, although it was often highly uncertain, an asterisk not an erasure.

Yet, even with the above approbation, I must offer a caveat. It is that post-modernism can be used, and no doubt was used, as an explanatory scheme that too often did within the arena of meaning, or hermeneutics, pretty much what the objective spectrum of ideology did in its curling back to the ideological right near the end of the spectrum. Part of the evidence for this is available in the actual political conduct of the post-modernists themselves. Hans-George Gadamer, a critic of modernism, continued to work in Germany throughout the Nazi period with barely a mention of his country's ongoing evil. Foucault, ostensibly such a cutting edge figure on the left, wound up admiring the Iranian Ayatollah and failed to question the Muslim fundamentalism that the post-Shah Iranian regime surely represented. There was more here of the objective left, and the psychological right, than a figure like Foucault ever allowed. And do not forget that the existentialist post-modern Martin Heidegger could not resist his attraction for Hitler, much to the horror of his friend Hannah Arendt. There was a play written about the two of them.

But apart from the sometimes latently conservative ideologies of at least some of the post-modernists, what I also suggest about them is that on the political side of what they were doing, at least in the United States which is the only place where I pretend to have any insight, intellectual post-modernism in the humanities and the social sciences frequently melded on college campuses with the de-centralizing political philosophy of the New Left, as well as the residual rigidity of so many, again not all, of the old socialisms. True conservatives, taking the classical, organic position of, say, an Edmund Burke, a Russell Kirk, or even a William F. Buckley, Jr. (or perhaps borrowing from an ancient Eastern figure like Confucius), were able to say with some truth that something that was less

than gentle, and something that was less than transcendent, afflicted so much of the radical left of the nineteen sixties and sev-
enties. A good deal of those absences came from the intellectual
arrogance of a philosophy, and its practitioners, that were, after
all, accessible to so few.

In short, what I am suggesting with my review of what I have labeled the false prophets is that none of the three perspectives I cite
in this chapter brought about the Natural Left, or the Psychological Left, as both an alternative to prior left of center ideologies, or
as what I believe to be the most credible ideology that will bring
structural and procedural equity to America's political system. In
short, none of the above positions provided for such equities and
their corresponding political entities, like parties, at a sub-atomic
level. Once more, the hard fact is that you don't get to the Natural
Left by indirection. You get to it when you prescribe for it.

You get to the Natural Left, to review, only when you place it
within the Dialectically Idealist, psychologically grounded, and
sub-atomically parsed sea marsh that specifically places the Natural Left's equity claim within the balances between preferences for
the different forms of understanding that are found within major
intellectual figures like Kant and Hegel. *For every objectivity, there
is a subjectivity* imports the subjective range. I repeat again that the
most discriminated against segment of the American polity in the
twenty-first century may increasingly be the citizen whose psychology is of the synthetic cognition. It is she whose perspective is
most excluded from the public sector in much the same way that
Barbara Ehrenreich and Susan Cain have described the exclusion of
the Jungian introverted type within the private sector.

A final point to conclude this chapter, and Part Two. If all of the
above sounds relativistic, please know that that relativism is intentional at the same time, I submit, that it is benign. Please be assured that what I utilize here is the more moderate, or "bounded"
form of relativity, wherein the number of perspectives is limited, not
infinite, and the *locus* of these relative points is known. I do not
advocate, or utilize, what is most frequently called "random" relativity, wherein the number of points is neither limited nor known,
and therefore prone to nihilism. I am talking about an acknowl-

edged, and limited, political and psychological spectrum, much like the relativity of the two human eyes that purposely create different cognitions, but operate together to deliver the third dimension in sight.

In sum, the political argument should not be any less insistent now for the subjectively diminished citizen than it was in the past for the objectively diminished citizen. As we on the left have struggled for the objective, whole, and cognitively undifferentiated groups that I have recognized above, girded by the principle that there are no second class Americans, I hope that our country, in the remaining eight and one-half decades of the twenty-first century, will demand equal political access for the citizen whose mind is of the synthetic cognition, and whose affective temperament is introverted, as Carl Jung understood it and as the insidious Myers-Briggs inventory tests for. Let us now move to Part Three and discuss how what we have talked about in Parts One and Two, that described and then hopefully deepened the theory's foundation, play out within the American political system.

References

Kate Fador, *Hannah and Martin*, Time Line Theater, Chicago, IL, 2003.

Michel Foucault, *Discipline and Punish: The Birth Of The Prison*, Paperback, New York, Vintage Press, 1995.

Tom Hayden, "The Port Huron Statement", Port Huron, MI, Students for a Democratic Society, 1962.

Theodore J. Lowi, *The End of Liberalism*, New York, W. W. Norton, 1969.

Jean-Francis Lyotard, *The Post-Modern Condition: A Report On Knowledge*, Paperback, Minneapolis, University of Minnesota Press, 1984.

C. Wright Mills, *The Power Elite*, London, Oxford University Press, 1956.

E. E. Schattschneider, *Party Government*, New York, Norton, 1942.

Part Three

American Political Inequity

Chapter Eleven

America's Legal Dialectic

In Parts One and Two I described an original political philosophy and then placed it within what I believed to be the richest possible intellectual framework for its development. In Part Three, made up of five short chapters, I will discuss a variety of traditional considerations, including America's only legal dialectic, its only political dialectic, its problems with campaign finance reform and political parties, America's place in the world and, finally, American politics' relationship to religion.

American political theory is not very abstract. Even more than the English who eschewed the lofty metaphysics of the French *philosophes* and preferred the empiricism of those like John Locke and David Hume, or even the didactic scolding of the skeptical Edmund Burke who responded to the pretentious French legislationists like Voltaire, Americans do not like, and have never created, much grand political philosophy. I mean no disrespect to the pragmatist writings of Charles Peirce, John Dewey, William James, or even the late Richard Rorty. But, sadly, I don't believe these writings get us to where we need to go. They do not make up anything like a theory of the Natural, or Psychological, Left.

If we are going to put our historical faith in an understanding of a cognitively alternating dialectic, then we should know, at least in retrospect, when it is that the dialectical elements occur, even if the contemporary participants may not recognize them at the time. In this chapter and the next I will share two examples of real world dialectics as I believe they occurred in American history. The legal example occurred largely in the Supreme Court of Chief Justice Earl Warren, although it included the years immediately preceding and following his tenure as well. The political example stretched itself out much longer, only the contradictory second dialectical phase occurring during the presidency of one of the two greatest American political figures, Abraham Lincoln, and, of course, the American Civil War.

The legal dialectic began slightly before the Warren Court, this Chief Justice being appointed shortly after the inauguration of president Dwight D. Eisenhower in January of 1953. The first dialectical case, which I may be alone in believing is the most important theoretical case in all of American jurisprudence, is *Shelley v. Kraemer* (1948). *Shelley* dealt with the issue of restrictive covenants in housing, the Supreme Court historically favoring such ostensibly private covenants when they included racial restrictions, although it had struck down a Kentucky state statute that racially discriminated against sales to minorities.

I also believe the *Shelley* case is mistaught in America's law schools. It is held to be a triumph for the public sector, the standard reasoning being that the enforcement of a restrictive covenant that prevented minorities from entering a neighborhood violated the Fourteenth Amendment's "state action" provision. The traditional interpretation concludes that the private sector covenant was therefore void. This reasoning, after all, is responsive to the way that NAACP General Counsel Thurgood Marshall had argued the case, and it is, to be sure, what the Supreme Court's opinion is based upon. Marshall, along with other activists of the time, wanted the Fourteenth Amendment's equal protection provision to assume a catalytic role in the development of a broad skein of legal opinions that would ostensibly rectify a number of social ills. They got it.

I see the case differently, guided in great part by the notion that just as in arguments between individuals, and just as in so many superficial political arguments, it is not theoretically correct to believe that the extant debate invariably represents the center of the controversy. I believe the private sector won, not lost, the *Shelley* case, wherein a white homeowner sold her home to a black family. Contrary to the traditional understanding, I believe that the main instrument of the case was the sales contract, not the covenant with which the neighborhood bigots would have prevented such a sale. What the restrictive covenant did, or attempted to do, was place an encumbrance on that contract. The covenant attempted to infuse an aberrant variable into an otherwise unencumbered, cognitively analytic, contract for the sale of a home. I would argue similarly that the covenant, signed by a significant number of homeowners in the neighborhood (although not the seller Ms. Fitzgerald), was the more public sector, synthetic document from the outset, aggregating the wishes of most of the community, as opposed to the wishes of two private, contracting individuals.

Finally, when looked at from a cognitive perspective, not only was the *Shelley v. Kraemer* case ruling a triumph for the analytic, not synthetic cognition, but, coming at a point when African-Americans (often former World War II soldiers although Shelley was a domestic factory worker during the War) sought to fulfill legitimate post-war expectations about their lives, Shelley asked for no more than to be able to enforce a contract that would triumph over the historical contradiction of treating African-Americans as citizens to be excluded. It was the prejudicially-inspired encumbrance of the restrictive covenant, the cognitively synthetic orange as it sought to intrude upon the apple-to-apple understanding of a bilateral contract, that sought to prevent the second stage dialectical contradiction from being addressed. This cognitively analytical ruling initiated the American legal dialectic at the same time that it demonstrated the limits of how far the analytic cognition and its attendant unencumbered contracts alone can carry a historical progress. The irony of the case, of course, is that the analytic cognition, almost invariably associated with a conservative political view, confronts a contract that is synthetic only at a purely substantive level, a white selling to a black. But again, that is what the first stage of the dialectic does. Its analytic *form* is what is important about it.

I argue the above with some confidence because the common law, more than anything else, was so much about the emergence of an increasingly unencumbered contract from various obstacles, beginning with the feudal entrapments of the millennium's early centuries, proceeding through the Stuart period's anti-common law reaction to Tudor commercialism, and eventually into those legislative encumbrances of which the conservative William Blackstone wrote so critically. I further submit that the American federalists' admonition against the impairing of the obligation of contract in Article One, Section Ten was one of the two key substantive provisions of a Constitution that was otherwise, as constitutions should be, overwhelmingly procedural. It was the core substantive provision of the Constitution, reflecting the tension between the federalists and the anti-federalists, the former preferring there to be no legislatively created encumbrances on a contract for debt, and the latter preferring the generous recognition of such encumbrances.

The other key provision of the Constitution, balancing Article One's admonition against impairing the contract, is the almost universally overlooked Seventh Amendment of the Bill of Rights. This amendment, barely mentioned in even full-sized law school textbooks, secured the inviolability of a jury determination of fact, the anti-federalist's response to Article One, Section Ten thus ensuring that the usually debtor-favorable fact finding that came from local juries would not be overturned by what were expected to be (and indeed became) federalist appellate court judges. Amidst all of the writings and rulings concerning the separation of powers, federalism, the commerce clause, and the other undeniably important procedural constructs within the Constitution, the core *substantive* controversy in the Constitution was between those who favored relatively unencumbered and those who favored relatively encumbered debt contracts. The procedural rules of the Constitution were never more than the rules of the game. They did not speak to the core ideological issue, the balance between the unencumbered, cognitively analytic, and the encumbered, cognitively synthetic, contract.

After *Shelley*, the dialectical sequence properly included several cognitively synthetic cases, they concerning the rights of the accused, the rights of minorities, the rights of gerrymandered voters, the rights of women, and so on. A traditional legal interpretation would label these cases, decided largely during Chief Justice Earl Warren's tenure, as activist. They judicially expanded the rule of law in meaningful areas. They did so without legislative initiation, often because of legislative obstruction. Of course, there had been four activist periods before Warren. But the John Marshall, Stephen

Field, W. H. Taft, and early Charles Evans Hughes courts all shifted the law to the conservative, and cognitively analytic, side. Let us briefly examine the synthetic cognitive nature of what I suggest are the three most important cases decided by the Warren Court.

Predictably, the first of what I argue are the most important synthetic, contradiction, or middle stage dialectical cases, is the *Brown v. Board of Education* case. Decided in 1954, the decision which held that segregated schools were inherently unequal rested on an extension of the Fourteenth Amendment's equal protection of the laws from a merely passive sense of equal *application* of the law, to the case's insistence that being a part of the larger society, socially, culturally, and educationally, was an *active* right worthy of constitutional protection. The case adds a variable, a qualitatively different, cognitively synthetic variable, to the legal mix as it deals with the contradiction of a nation founded on a standard of public sector equality but still denying equal educational opportunity to some. All of this was still a part of the larger society nearly two centuries after the founding. The *Brown* case transforms a common law, merely private sector sense of equity, which could still include separation, into a public right to be a full member of the life of the community. Of course it uses the cognitively synthetic form.

Another case that unmistakably relied upon the introduction of a cognitively synthetic variable is *Baker v. Carr* (1962). The rationale underlying this case's decision was not wholly dissimilar from *Brown*, the case holding that a voter was entitled to have her vote weighted more or less equally with every other voter. Prior to *Baker*, the issue of whether or not a citizen was fairly represented was ruled a "political question," and thus open only to legislative, not judicial, remedy. But *Baker* held that it was not enough that we all have to stop at a stop sign. It held that we all get to decide where the stop sign should be placed. The succeeding reapportionment cases that dealt with contrivances that impeded the goal of equal representation like the County Unit System in Georgia, and even the malapportionment of state upper houses, employed the same logic. They all enforced a standard of public, political equity, the fair apportionment of votes in electoral districts. The introduction of that new standard was cognitively synthetic.

The final cognitively synthetic case (of the three that may best represent the dialectical nature of the Earl Warren Supreme Court) deals with the still much-debated case of *Roe v. Wade* (1973), a case decided four years after Chief Justice Warren left the court. Here, as with *Shelley v. Kraemer*, a sub-atomic analysis lends a different interpretation from the standard interpretation. *Roe* is traditionally held to be a privacy case, with the insularity of the woman protected by the court's ruling that the decision not to carry a pregnancy to term is hers alone. In the everyday meaning of the term, privacy indeed means what it says. But a cognitively derived, sub-atomic understanding of the case reveals a triumph for the public sector, as well as a triumph for the public's multiplicity of choice over the diminution of that choice to a singular, in this case religiously dictated, imperative. Perhaps less obviously but in some ways more dramatically than even *Brown* or *Baker*, *Roe*, after all, insists upon a cognitive complexity. It is cognitively synthetic, again in the contradictory, middle dialectic stage way, as are so many of the other Warren era cases. Again, that dialectical period did indeed slightly outlast Earl Warren himself on the court, with the Richard Nixon appointed Associate Justice Harry Blackmun writing an opinion with which the Warren Court's residual liberals readily agreed. Nixon was not pleased.

To conclude this summary of America's sole legal dialectic, I offer an interpretation of an analytic case, one of many others that I'm sure could be cited as completing the three-stage, cognitively alternating periods of decision that are emblematic of the Supreme Court's dialectical experience. The wave had passed. Warren and his brethren, and to at least some degree the great controversies over the social and political issues that they faced, had passed as well. The new, more conservative court, the court of the next Supreme Court Chief Justice Warren Burger, gloried in its thermidor period with cases like *Richmond v. Croson* (1989).

In the city of Richmond, Virginia the newly elected, African-American majority government had initiated "set-asides" for minority contractors as an affirmative action recompense for years of anti-black discrimination. These set asides were broad brush in their application, open to all who were of the race, not just those who had suffered prior contracting discrimination. The Burger Court said "no" to that sweep, requiring that only claimants who had previously been discriminated against for contracts under white-dominated administrations could seek the restitution of set-asides. Rulings of this kind, restricting the claim to those who would have contracted earlier, are clearly of the analytic cognitive form. And thus we have the third stage of the American legal dialectic. The Warren Court, accompanied both before and after by but a few years and fewer cases, is the sole fully three-stage dialectic in all American jurisprudence.

I should also point out that the English law once experienced a similar three-stage dialectical pattern, it coming at a point in English commercial and democratic development that greatly facilitated the later American understandings of democracy's requirements. The key player in the English dialectic was Sir Edward Coke, the second stage of his dialectic (I'll get to the first shortly) being typified by such confrontations with the Stuart kings as *Dr. Bonham's Case* (1610), so essential for the development of judicial review and cited in *The Federalist Papers*. Similarly, in *The Ecclesiastical Cases* (1616), the notions of political representation are advanced by Coke's references to the will of the flock in clerical appointments in another argument with the first James. In The Petition of Right (1628), Coke successfully reasserted the supremacy of law over government, and pointedly, the crown, in this case Charles I. The third English dialectical stage took place in the next century wherein Sir William Blackstone's multi-volume Commentaries attempted to defend the inner decisional calculus of the common law against that "ten times a larger bulk" of statues that we mentioned earlier, he feeling such statutes had contaminated the common law. Blackstone completed the principal English dialectic.

I intentionally left the first stage for last in the English dialectic discussion because it came about in a case that I find to be almost perfectly matched to the *Shelley v. Kraemer* case that I find so important to American jurisprudence. The case was decided in 1581, at the height of the Elizabethan period wherein the common law, with its contract and property notions, was achieving the bloom that the historian Henry Maine labeled as the transition of modernity from status to contract. Coke had been a member of the bar for but two years when one brother sold land to a third party in a way that quite probably violated the traditional feudal encumbrances on the land of that time. But with Coke's arguments the good faith third party purchaser of the land, without notice, shed the encumbrances. The sale held. The case's title? *Shelley's Case*, naturally.

In sum, my reason for emphasizing the *form* of the legal dialectic in this chapter is quite simple. In America, after four periods of judicial activism that favored the private sector, cognitively analytic position, exercised almost invariably in the protection of property and the unencumbered contract, the Earl Warren Court, again with a slight overlap both before and after Justice Warren's tenure, was active for the first time in the other ideological, sectoral, and cognitive, direction. Of course, a) the conservative John Marshall court directly following the founding that introduced judicial review so as to permit judicial protection of the contract, b) the Stephen Field court that created (out of thin air) a legal notion called substantive due process in order to protect robber baron-era private arrangements in the late nineteenth century, c) the William Howard Taft court that struck down some progressive era legislation, and d) the early Charles Evans Hughes court that struck down so much of Franklin Roosevelt's first term New Deal legislation, were all activist. But each of them, again, was active on the cognitively analytic, private sector, and politically conservative, side of the ledger.

I argue, of course, that the Earl Warren court's activism, which protected and even expanded the public rights of citizens, using the synthetic cognition if not consciously doing so, was every bit as legitimate in its judicial rule-making as were the four conservative court activisms. A cognitively balanced standard for judge-made law will include a sense of where each cognition belongs in the alternating cognitions of America's sole legal dialectic. The American study of the English common law, the essence of which I maintain a certain affection for even with its biases, need not preclude the utilization of interpretive methodologies that go beyond the English common law method. Because the classical, that is philosophical foundation, has not been taught typically in America's law schools does not mean that we cannot begin to teach it, with great benefit, in the future. The substance of the English common law can be greatly enriched by an interpretative hybrid, although the ingenuous interpretative assumption of American law schools since their inception has never reached anything like it. The forms, and the dialectic that is their necessary product, can co-exist with the common law, even if that option has inexplicably been left unexplored. Let us next examine the sole American political dialectic.

References

Baker v. Carr, 369 U. S. 549, (1962).

Dr. Bonham's Case, 8 Co. Rep. 114 (Court of Common Pleas [1610]).

Brown v. The Board of Education of Topeka, Kansas, 347 U. S. 483, (1954).

Roe v. Wade, 410 U. S. 113, (1973).

Shelley v. Kraemer, 334 U. S. 1, (1948).

Shelley's Case, 1 Co. Rep. 93b, 76 Eng. Rep. 206 (C.P.) (1581).

William Blackstone, *Commentaries,* (New York: Augustus M. Kelley, 1969).

For The Ecclesiastical Cases, see James Harvey Robinson, *Readings in European History,* (Boston: Ginn & Co. 1906, 2, 221–223.

For the Petition of Right, see J. P. Kenyon, *The Stuart Constitution,* 1603–1866, Documents and Commentary, (Cambridge: Cambridge university Press, 1986).

Chapter Twelve

America's Political Dialectic

The notion of the dialectic embraces those rare but pivotal historical moments during which a fundamental conflict is both faced and, for better or worse, resolved. In all of the varied literature about the American Civil War, the one constant is that this moment in our country's history marked the decisive determining of the one issue that the Philadelphia founders had put aside as a deal breaker: slavery. Of course, accompanying issues—like those surrounding federalism, tariffs, and even the anglophilic bias of the Southern aristocracy that is only hinted at in most textbooks—all entered into the mix of high emotion that led to the terrible War.

On June 16, 1858, Abraham Lincoln stood in what is now the Old Capital in Springfield, Illinois and gave one of the most important political speeches in our nation's history. In that "House Divided" address, Lincoln argued that America had come to a crossroads wherein a definitive political choice must be made. Smarting from what he saw as the increasing diminution of the national jurisdiction, Lincoln began by saying "If we could first know *where* we are, and *whither* we are tending, we could then better judge *what* to do, and *how* to do it" (emphases his).

For Lincoln, an incremental rending of the union was increasingly inevitable, due in no small part to the Fugitive Slave Act of 1850, the Kansas-Nebraska "popular sovereignty" Act of 1854, the 1857 *Dred Scott* case's holdings that African Americans were not federal citizens and that the federal government could not allocate slave and free statuses in the territories, all of these in the shadow of John C. Calhoun's plea for a concurrent, or veto-like, majority rule in federal legislation. Calhoun's requirement of a pseudo-majority, of course, would have returned our country to the state-sovereign position of the Articles of Confederation. All of the above events, linked with the weak and slavery-sympathetic presidencies of Franklin Pierce and James Buchanan, led Lincoln to reason that if the bleeding did not stop, the patient, the national government, would surely die. A historical contradiction was at hand, the above events thus far being overwhelmingly analytic.

A civil war is probably the grandest of all national contradictions. The English Civil War was much a milestone in that country's history, while the American Civil War still accounts for more combat deaths, and more discussion, than all of our other wars combined. Surely, America's Civil War was far more costly than the synthetic contradictions that eventually led to, and were so much a part of, legal cases like *Brown*, although *Brown's* prelude certainly included the violence and loss of life that often accompanied being an African-American in the United States. The voter discriminations that preceded the *Baker* case entailed political exclusion, and the *Roe* case was just as assuredly preceded by the extreme discomfort, even death, of so many women being forced into back alley abortions. But nothing is as terrible, as contradictory, as war.

The contradiction between an eighteenth century, aristocratic society—one that resisted the political complexities of industrialization, urbanization, and the immigrations of a foreign born, non-Anglo Saxon working class on one side—and a nineteenth century society that embraced the above modernities even if it was anything but wholly free of racial bias, on the other, was clearly dialectical. Two centuries fought in the American Civil War. In a Chicago speech one month after the more famous Springfield oration, Lincoln responded to a Stephen Douglas attack on the Springfield talk that accused Lincoln of using the dialectic. The charge, coming precisely ten years after the publication of Marx's *Manifesto*, had more than the usual sting of foreignness attached to it —a kind of a philosophical birth certificate challenge.

In response, Lincoln dissembled "I have not a fine education. I am not capable of entering into a disquisition upon dialectics, as I believe you call it; but I do believe the language I employed bears any such construction as Judge Douglas put upon it." As with the legal dialectic, it is something of a crap shoot as to exactly when the reconciliative, analytic, third phase took place after the political contradiction. One could argue for the Civil Rights Act of 1964 and the Voting Rights Act of 1965, finally guaranteeing something like full political and economic citizenship to the African American citizen. But one might equally argue that the reconciliation of the third political stage for African-Americans is still neither complete nor secure, particularly with the kind of Supreme Court ruling that recently abrogated a core Voting Rights Act section.

In the summer of 2007, I attended the American Political Science Association meeting in Chicago and sat in on a panel that included a staunch conservative from the University of Maryland Law School by the name of Mark A. Graber. Graber had recently written a book entitled *Dred Scott and the Problem of Constitutional Evil*, and though he did not reference a cognitive, much less dialectical, model of understanding, he did vigorously argue that the historical contradiction that Lincoln spoke to, and later acted upon, was neither obvious nor imperative. Graber did not suggest that *Dred Scott* was good law, nor did he suggest for a moment that the other pre-War diminutions of federal authority were good for the divided nation. But he did contend that Lincoln's notion of a necessary climax at a moment of history was contrived. He went on to note that throughout history, ambitious political figures had frequently claimed that a crossroads moment had arisen, and that bold and decisive action from a freshly empowered political figure was therefore imperative, usually under the guidance of that same figure who proclaimed the arrival of the historical fork in the road.

In the overall, I take Prof. Graber's point seriously, even as my underlying ideological perspective is much at variance with his. History surely records far too many aspiring, and too often successful, tyrants who have assigned themselves a dialectical role in history, falsely claiming that they acted at a point in time wherein nothing less than a dramatic and bold restructuring of the political order was necessary. But granting Prof. Graber's general point, I nonetheless disagree with Graber's specifics as they relate to the greatest American conflict. I further suggest that our country may now be at another point of significant contradiction, that contradiction witnessing our country's confronting of an emerging, and converging, world order. I will discuss this contradiction specifically in Chapter Fourteen, following a discussion of campaign finance reform and political parties in the next chapter.

In the remainder of this chapter, however, I will attempt to explain at least one of the underlying reasons for why I think the relative fortunes of our country have declined precipitously over the last years, as evidenced by our still growing debts, our continued trade deficits (up to $39.1 billion in July of 2013), the reduction in our bond rating, the loss of our educational primacy, and the deterioration of America's infrastructure. Yes, the combination of a slightly improved economy, large Fanny Mae and Freddy Mac payments, and the tax avoidance early tax payments of 2012 recently shrunk the deficits slightly and gave us a window of roughly three years to do the budgetary work that must be done. But then the trend line shoots upward again. We've fallen a long way and I suggest that what has happened in large part reflects the inability of America's government to recalibrate itself in a moderate but effective fashion and revisit the structural equilibriums that are necessary for a vibrant and just government, as well as a government that guides us through the twenty-first century's historical transition.

Recently, two knowledgeable books have appeared that are the product of political scientists who have been concerned with the calamity of our government for some time. The first, entitled *It's Even Worse Than It Looks: How the American Constitutional System Collided With the New Political Extremism*, was co-authored by Thomas E. Mann and Norman J. Ornstein, two of America's finest students of the Congress. The second, *Towards A More Perfect Constitution*, was written by Larry Sabato, whose decades of study of the American government are well chronicled in his books and articles, as well as in his thoughtful media appearances. Both these works describe serious, systemic problems with the American government in detail, again these becoming so precipitous, I believe, because of America's inability to deal with the demands of an ever more competitive world.

To be sure, attention to the systemic problems of the American government is not new. As long ago as the nineteen fifties, Rexford

Tugwell, a member of the FDR brain trust, joined with a number of similarly concerned citizens and made recommendations for the improvement of the government. There were also two Hoover (Herbert, not J. Edgar) Commissions in the post-war period, each suggesting institutional improvements in the political system, although at a sub-constitutional level. The most extensive review of our political system was undertaken by a group that called itself the Committee on the Constitutional System, it doing its work in the early to mid-nineteen eighties and submitting its report to the President and the Congress in January, 1987. I played some role in the formation of that group, my U.S. Senate campaign in 1980 calling for a constitutional review of the world's most centrifugal government to coincide with the document's bicentennial. My plea was heard by the dean of American political journalists at the time: Richard Strout. Strout wrote of my campaign in his TRB column of *The New Republic* and in a piece in *The Christian Science Monitor*. I publicly sought the assistance of anyone who wished to form a constitutional study group and was happy to receive a call from the late political scientist Charles M. Hardin, a Harvard Ph.D. who taught many years at the University of Chicago. Hardin, who had written extensively about gridlock in the American government, cobbled together what became CCS.

Seventeen citizens, mostly academics, met first at the DuPont Plaza Hotel in Washington's DuPont Circle in January of 1981, under the direction of Prof. Hardin. The group grew to over one hundred within two years, and came to be chaired by former White House counsel Lloyd Cutler, former Secretary of the Treasury C. Douglas Dillon, (who financed and attended the DuPont Plaza gathering) and the former United States Senator Nancy Kassebaum, (R-KS). Noted political figures like former Senator J. William Fulbright (D-AK), the former chair of the Joint Economic Committee of the Congress Henry Reuss (D-WI), and broad gauge academics like Gerhard Casper, then Dean of the University of Chicago Law School who went on to become president of Stanford University, Duke's Walter Dellinger, who was shortly to be the Attorney General of the United States, the Brookings Institution's James L. Sundquist, who had written extensively on the American constitutional order for many years, along with Donald Robinson at Smith College and James MacGregor Burns at Williams College, were representative of the more active and richly contributing members of our group. People have been kind enough to say that I contributed a mite to the discussion as well. Let me summarily review the more important of CCS's proposals, and then discuss the specific issue of campaign finance reform in somewhat greater detail, from a cognitive perspective. I will conclude by commenting on what I believe to be the failings of America's two large political parties.

Let it be clear that CCS's principal theme, like the main theme of my 1980 Senatorial campaign, revolved around the need to rebalance the centralizing and decentralizing energies in the American constitutional order. There was unanimous agreement within this diverse group of participants that the American political system had fragmented even beyond the founders' original centrifugal design, and that the pieces had to be pulled together if the citizenry was to receive effective government. The most salient and universally agreed upon of CCS's proposals was the extension of the House of Representatives term from two years to four years, the term to run concurrently with the presidential term. A requirement that a sitting House member would need to resign from the lower house should she wish to run for the Senate at the midpoint of her term would, of course, be necessary if Senate approval for such an amendment would have any chance at passage.

We of CCS felt that the severe fragmenting of America's government that had begun to evidence itself in the 1970's could best be countered by giving the members of Congress's lower house some respite from the by then constant fund-raising and campaigning that television advertising and jet airplane travel back to the district had made almost mandatory. Although our discussions did not dwell for long on how the gridlock in government had come about, mention of the original decentralized arrangement of the Constitution was supplemented by discussion of the overly decentralizing sub-constitutional "reforms," as above, that the so-called "Class of '74" had inflicted on the national legislature. The newly won independence of committees and sub-committees, along with restrictions on multiple chairships discussed above, along with

other burdens on institutional integrity, all contributed to the gridlock, the growing budget deficits, the trade deficits, and the chronic
up-ticks in the national debt that now approaches seventeen trillion
dollars. When I first ran for the Senate in 1980, not incidentally,
the national debt was nine hundred and forty-two billion dollars,
the annual deficit being $63 billion. A recent forecast predicts a
twenty trillion dollar deficit by the year 2019. Even with the promised
three year "window" of smaller deficits, that prediction might be conservative.

Another CCS recommendation was that Section Six of the Constitution's Article One be amended to permit members of the Congress to serve concurrently at the cabinet or sub-cabinet level of
the executive branch. Our constitution, recall, prescribes not only
for the separation of powers. It prescribes as well for the separation of people, a further decentralizing linchpin in the protection
against "factions" that the Philadelphia founders, as written about
favorably in James Madison's *Federalist* #10, so feared.

CCS also made lesser recommendations, the reduction of the
treaty approval requirement to a simple majority from its two-
thirds constitutional requirement being something the venerable
Jim Sundquist at Brookings had always felt strongly about. Jim re-
membered the Senate struggle over the Treaty of Versailles from his
childhood, and he still mourned the devastating failure of the League
of Nations that may have been averted by American participation.

CCS also approved Jim Burns' notion of a "team ticket," a de-
vice by which a voter could pull one lever to include all federal candidates of the same party. On the other hand, a proposal to permit
a European-style, legislative vote of "no confidence" was rejected
by a single vote in perhaps the most vigorous of all CCS debates. I
voted with the majority, not solely because I thought the no confidence vehicle wouldn't fit into our system (the argument most
prominently made on the negative side), but because I believed
that the institution of the no confidence vote was in fact *inversely*
related to the otherwise centripetal arrangements of the European
parliamentary systems. The no confidence vote, in my view, is really an escape valve in parliamentary countries like the United King-
dom that have tightly integrated political institutions. Its relationship

to the system entire is complementary, not direct. Standing alone in our far more scattered system, it would only wreak further havoc, or so I thought. It was interesting to me that, of all the able people who spoke to the issue of the vote of no confidence, not one considered the possibility that the relationship of such a vote to the overall system might be inverse. Linear minds, I was learning, are not comfortable with inverse relationships, and inverse relationships are structurally synthetic.

CCS also discussed the parliamentary institution of "question time," wherein the chief executive is subjected to queries by the legislative body, in our case the Congress, though it did not include this notion within its recommendations. Notably, Republican candidate John McCain in America's 2008 presidential election offered his willingness to be questioned periodically by the Congress. The idea was covered by the press, for a day.

In sum, although the deliberations of CCS were surely atheoretical, I am happy to say that the participants in that group, made up nearly equally of "persons of affairs" and academics, did seem to have at least a visceral understanding that the necessary business of our country, if not the progress of our country in a very different historical age, required a critical mass of coherent political structures. If there was not an out and out dialectician in the house, well maybe one, there were at least some very smart and experienced people in the CCS meetings. In my judgment, their recommendations would have been of significant value had they been put into effect. In fact, I don't believe that the bias against the synthetic cognition in the American political system will be remedied until proposals like those of CCS are taken seriously. I will discuss my own ideas in a subsequent chapter. But the record thus far is that neither of the two major American political parties has paid any attention to CCS's recommendations. The current need for structural change has thus far been wholly ignored, and our country continues to suffer the consequences.

References

Mark A. Graber, *Dred Scott and the Problem of Constitutional Evil,* Cambridge, Cambridge University Press, 2006.

Abraham Lincoln, "Speech at Chicago, Illinois," in *Abraham Lincoln: Speeches and Writings,* Roy P. Basler, ed., New York, The Library of America, 1989.

Thomas E. Mann and Norman J. Ornstein, *It's Even Worse Than It Looks — How the American Constitutional System Collided With the New Politics of Extremism,* New York, Basic Books, 2012.

Larry Sabato, *Towards A More Perfect Constitution,* New York, Walker and Company, 2007.

Dred Scott v. Sandford, 60 U. S. (39 Howard) 393, 1857.

Chapter Thirteen

Campaign Finance and Political Parties

Beyond constitutional considerations, and beyond the lessons of America's legal and political constitutional history, it must be acknowledged that many of the deepest cognitive disequilibria within the American political system do not exist at the constitutional level. They exist at the sub-constitutional level and not only within the legislative or executive branches and their internal arrangements. A review of both the way our country finances its political campaigns and the way its parties operate should further our understanding of America's current political malady. In addition to CCS's constitutional-level recommendations, incidentally, a number of sub-constitutional suggestions were included in CCS' final report. The most important concerned campaign finance reform, something I wrote about in an Issue Brief for the American Constitution Society. It is available in the "Democracy and Voting" section of ACS —October 2007, or by Googling my name. Long before the horrific decision in *Citizens United v. F.E.C.* (2010), the Supreme Court had begun its impeding of meaningful campaign finance reform in the 1976 case of *Buckley v. Valeo*. A conservative majority in that case held that although individual contributions to a political candidate could be regulated by Congress, the expenditure of a political candidate's own money, and the independent expenditure of citizens or groups who support a candidate without coordination with the campaign, were protected under the free speech provisions of the First Amendment. The constitutional separation of contributions and expenditures, the former being available for regulation and the latter not, was something that Associate Justice

Byron "Whizzer" White was alone in finding to be wholly specious. I agreed with Justice White then, and I still do.

Traditional arguments over campaign finance spending center around the conflating of First Amendment protections of speech with the expenditures of money on campaigns. The recently retired Justice John Paul Stevens has argued that this conflation is also highly specious. I agree wholeheartedly with Justice Stevens but my principal argument, unlike Stevens's, rests beyond the First Amendment. It rests in a cognitive analysis of the Bill of Rights entire.

Though it is often misunderstood, in part because of right-wing propaganda which has argued that the Bill of Rights stands solely for individual and "negative" rights (those that keep the government from doing something to you), the fact is that the Bill of Rights stands for collective, that is political rights, thus guaranteeing that you along with your fellow citizens are entitled, positively, to do things that impact your government. To better understand this notion, let us briefly review the Bill of Rights amendments.

Apart from the two religious provisions in the First Amendment (both of which complemented rather than detracted from the "no religious test" provision of the federalists' Article Six), the protections of free speech, a free press, petition, and the right of association in the First Amendment all were designed to ensure aggregational, or group, activity. The Second Amendment's gun protection, vastly overblown in its importance by the right and grossly misunderstood in a recent Supreme Court case that extended gun rights to individuals beyond a state militia, ensured the protection of states and their militias from a tyrannous national government. The Third Amendment's protection against soldiers bedding in private homes removed the eyes and ears of the government from places where oppositional activity might be taking place, while the search and seizure protection of the Fourth Amendment was designed to ward off intelligence gathering by a sitting government concerning conjoined opposition.

The Fifth Amendment's procedural protections of not having to tattle on oneself, and the Sixth Amendment's guarantee of counsel and a speedy trial protected against politically motivated criminal prosecutions. The Eighth Amendment's protection against cruel and unusual punishment, we often forget, was not solely retrospective; like the rest of the Bill of Rights, it was prospective in its forbidding of the kinds of questioning techniques, read torture, which would elicit information about political accomplices, along with plans for political contradiction.

The "sleeper" in the Bill of Rights, as I began to discuss in the last chapter, is the Seventh Amendment, which protects the fact-findings of a federal jury against what were anticipated to be, and what became, federalist appellate court judges. Again, the Seventh Amendment is hardly worthy of more than a mention in most textbooks but in fact it is centrally important to the overturning of *Buckley v. Valeo's* and subsequent cases' (*Citizens United*) restrictions on campaign reform. In concert with the Third Article's inclusion of the considerations of equity along with the law, as well as Alexander Hamilton's concession in *Federalist* #80 regarding the common law "hard bargain" (and of course the Third Article's inclusion of the equity jurisdiction which would permit a judge to find for the debtor by placing an encumbrance on an unfair, creditor-favoring contract), the Seventh Amendment's protection of what a local (presumably more debtor favorable) jury would find permitted an encumbering of a contract in the same way that legislation might protect a debtor from unfair contracts.

Above all, in discussing the ideological balance between the original seven articles of the Constitution and the subsequent Bill of Rights, let us remember the grand irony contained in the American Constitution. That irony is that although the *locus* (or place) of the first seven articles of the Constitution resides in specific governmental or public institutions, the *telos*, or purpose, of the Constitution's first seven articles resides in its protection of the private sector. The substantive essence of the Philadelphia founders' work, as discussed above, was to protect the unencumbered contract. Conversely, whereas the *locus* of the amendments in the Bill of Rights rests with the individual—specifically the individual citizen's right to speak, petition, pamphleteer, etc.—the *telos*, or purpose, of the Bill of Rights is to protect public sector, oppositional political activity, this grand constitutional irony not always being well understood.

Chapter Ten's review of the federalists' and anti-federalists' very differing political and juridical perspectives, along with the Constitution's Article One, Section Ten protection of the unencumbered contract and along with the balancing Seventh Amendment's protection of a jury's encumbering of a contract, can deal with the problem of the large campaign contribution. Such a contribution, whether bundled within one entity to make up that contribution, or spent independently through a "527" association, or even given to a campaign by the candidate itself, is not a contribution at all. It is, in fact, a contract. Just as importantly, it is, in its form and substance, an unencumbered contract. It contains an expectation of a specific political return for a so-called contribution. Unencumbered contracts, and particularly politically influencing political contracts from wealthy and powerful interests, were never intended to be protected by the Bill of Rights.

Put another way, the unencumbered, I believe falsely named, "contribution" contrasts qualitatively and not just quantitatively with the small contribution that is invariably encumbered, as it is understood by its giver to be soon commingled with other contributions. The unencumbered contribution, or contract, is in direct conflict with the purpose of the anti-federalists who sought to advance the interests of the yeoman citizen and did so in the small "d" democratic spirit of the Bill of Rights, this in opposition to the aristocratic spirit of the original seven articles. The synthetic cognition, which makes up the second, or contradictory, stage of the dialectic, cannot be generated in American politics when the unencumbered, contractually formed relationship between single issue interest groups and the government prevents both comprehensive legislation in a variety of policy areas, as well as the kinds of structural and procedural change that might rebalance the American political order.

Seen in the light of the above cognitively-driven perspective, *Buckley v. Valeo* was simply wrong. Subsequent cases that have built on *Buckley* and have protected political activity like the falsely represented "issue advertising," or have struck down the "millionaire's amendment" that allowed compensatory public financing for those who ran against the wealthy, only made the situation worse. The "capstone" case, as some lawyers refer to an inevitable ruling that marks the conclusion to a series of single direction cases, is *Citizens United v. F.E.C.*, it fully equating a corporation with a person, and opening the floodgates for a corporate torrent of contributions. If public financing for elections is not to be had, a case that reverses *Buckley* and the more recent *Citizens United* is absolutely imperative for a return to America's constitutional democracy. I immodestly submit that the legal argument I advance here is the most robust available for the overturning of *Buckley* and *Citizens United*. Yes, the Supreme Court has, as per Justice Stevens, misunderstood the essence of the free speech provision of the First Amendment. But in a larger sense, the Supreme Court has misunderstood the essence of the Bill of Rights, particularly its complementary ideological, and *cognitive*, place in contradistinction to the original seven articles. That misunderstanding must be corrected. Let us turn now to the theoretical, cognitively centered, context of America's increasingly unrepresentative major political parties.

I have come to the point in my thinking about America's national political parties where I believe that the one-time robust New York state practice of having two and two-half significant parties is the optimum party configuration for our country. Each half party should act as an "outrigger," something that represents a clear ideological alternative to the two major parties, as did the New York Liberal and Conservative parties. Two great maladies currently afflict the American two party system. One is incumbency. The assurance that congressional members will be reelected without serious opposition because their districts have been uncompetitively drawn because of bi-partisan collusion has left far too many House of Representatives districts without serious opposition. The Senate, although there is an occasional surprise within a party's primary vote, is even more impervious to revisions in its personnel. Such incumbency only increases the likelihood that public office holders will engage, over time, in the analytic form of contractual relationships with powerful lobbyists and constituents. Naturally, the synthetic form of public policy generation, not to mention the necessary adaptations for America's coming political challenges, suffers the consequences.

The second American party malady is legislative collusion. Just as Adam Smith presciently warned about the proclivity of economic interests to combine in order to fix prices, share markets, and so forth, the two major American parties have grown far too comfortable with each other on a variety of core public issues. The passage of the inequitable and fiscally irresponsible George W. Bush tax cuts, the deprivations of basic liberties within the Patriot Act and, above all, the authorization for the Iraqi War when Senator Carl Levin's (D-MI) amendment on United Nations involvement was available to avoid the decision, are only the most recent, and most glaring, examples of inter-party collusion. Even the lame duck 2010 session in the days before Christmas evidenced far greater collusion than the press wanted to report, the tax compromise resting solely on a two-party agreement to make the budget deficit even worse than it already was.

Not incidentally, intra-party collusion is rife within the two Big Box parties as well. Hillary Clinton just plain lied in a Democratic primary debate when she said that American sovereignty would have been surrendered if Senator Levin's sending the war issue to the United Nations Security Council had passed the Congress. For this, she was vigorously criticized by the mainstream press but that same pro-Obama press declined to mention that the gentleman sitting three feet away from Senator Clinton at the debate surely knew she had lied but chose to smile rather than speak. At the conclusion of the debate, the two Democratic presidential candidates from Illinois locked arms and shared an adoring gaze, secure in their belief that they had fooled most of the people, at least for a time, and that was good enough for now. They didn't fool me.

I might point out, by the way, that as deplorable as the above *pas de deux* was between then Senators Clinton and Obama, it paled in comparison to the political pandering of the individual whom presidential nominee Obama wound up choosing as his Vice Presidential running mate. The inestimable Joseph Biden of Delaware reached a modern low in American presidential campaigning with not one but two blatantly neo-Confederate pronouncements in Columbia, SC in the early summer of 2008. "I'm from a slave state, too" he intoned, following up with "[i]f there hadn't been two states be-tween us, we would have been down here to help you", words that remain unrepudiated by the Vice President even though he received correspondence on it from the principal drafter of the national De-mocratic Party charter who is also an active member of the Sons of Union Veterans whose great grandfather was shot in November, 1864 outside Franklin, Tennessee. Biden is too dim a bulb to have considered that an SUVCW member might have been blocks from his Columbia speech, and he has lacked the courage, or the cour-tesy, to return to Columbia, and acknowledge that the city that en-dured its burning in 1865 at the hands of both Confederate and Union soldiers, my wife's great grandfather riding with Hampton's Legion, did not need that horrible memory to be revived by a politi-cian whose ambition was matched by neither his intellect nor his judgment. I should add that Columbia, SC is also the home of Rep-resentative Joe Wilson, who embarrassed our country before the world by shouting "you lie" at President Obama in his first State of the Union address after Biden's Columbia speech. Was Rep. Wilson emboldened by now Vice President Biden's remarks? Was the South Carolina House of Representatives so emboldened when it recently voted to nullify, that's right — nullify, the Affordable Care Act? The good and loyal citizens of South Carolina do not deserve an appeal to a tiny sliver of neo-Confederate opinion that only embarrasses their state and emboldens the worst element within it.

Collusion between and within the two principal parties is the key to understanding another arena wherein American democracy falls short. If the most powerful corporate interests give money to both parties, as this nation's private sector now increasingly does, is it any wonder that the two major parties respond to their patrons sim-ilarly? Is it any wonder either that tax breaks for the oil industry, tax breaks for the hedge fund industry, the almost wholesale destruc-tion of a progressive taxation instrument like the estate tax, along with the secular decline of the corporate share of the overall tax bur-den, continue to seem impermeable to public outrage? To be fair, the president has spoken out on these issues, but thus far to no avail.

Some argue that the American political system generally, and the Congress specifically, engage in far too much partisanship. I don't believe it. Partisanship, even the idiocy of the Tea Party which I believe to now be in the eclipse, is the essence of democracy and the United States government has too little, not too much of it. A good part of the reason that there appears to be more partisanship than some citizens wish for is that an enormous backlog of pressing public issues has built up over time. Our country's next generation faces a myriad of problems in education, infrastructure, housing, long term unemployment, not to mention the long term funding of Medicare, Medicaid, Social Security, and the over one hundred trust funds that have been looted as a result of the "unified budget" that Lyndon Johnson created when he could not responsibly fund the Viet Nam War.

Most importantly, how does our political system handle the national debt? How is this country, even with a temporary respite from crushing annual deficits and with the admittedly successful small scale spending reductions that the president has achieved, going to break through our gridlock and solve the long term budget shortfall? The conversation over these issues has hardly been too loud; the solutions, even after the most recent political campaigns, are limited to things like a health care law that throws thirty million more Americans into the maw of the insurance industry, and at the same time risked being declared unconstitutional, (as part of it eventually was), as well as opened an avenue, used by Chief Justice John Roberts, for novel restrictions on the Commerce Clause. Yes, I certainly approve of getting rid of the doughnut hole, the annual caps, the pre-existing conditions, as well as the inclusion of mental difficulties, but wouldn't it have been both easier and more inclusive if we had done single payer, or Medicare for all? Some early reports on exchange health insurance costs are encouraging but will it last? The president has already raised fees for some consumers, for selected insurers, and never forget what Adam Smith said about the readiness to "combine" among businesses. To be fair to Obama, the political system itself was partly to blame for the inability to pass single payer. But I smile at the certitude that both arguing sides now claim for the workability or non-workability of the Act. It will be years before we know whether we have truly bent the curve on health care costs, and specifically whether the insurance companies can circumvent the caps that seem at first to restrict insurance company gouging. Throw in the financial regulation bill, Dodd-Frank, that left so many of its protocols to Wall Street authorship that no one knows whether the final product will help or harm the consumer, and the Obama legislative record is iffy, at best. Again, to be fair, the fault lies partly with a political system that cannot synthesize majoritarian citizenry requests.

And though it's true that the Republican Party has generated the greatest recent assault on our nation's fiscal health, its wage and tax equity, and even its strategic security (by beginning wars that more often strengthen our enemies than defeat them), it has been the Democratic Party, charged on the synthetic half of the cognitive spectrum with the obligation to respond to the analytic half, that has too often abandoned its historical Jefferson/Jackson/Roosevelt commitment to abstain from all too cozy relationships with corporate politics. Has the Democratic Party, even its well intentioned members of which there are still a few, rescued the American middle class from its declining condition? No. The Gini Coefficient continues to increase, the gaps in both income and wealth growing larger. I recommend the writings of observers like Robert Reich, who remind us that the top 1% of American earners now accounts for nearly 20% of all national income while that same 1% accounts for fully 35% of all national wealth. Reich puts it bluntly: these inequalities have been "created." They did not just occur.

So in closing, let us remember, first, that the Democratic Party did not do one thing to respond to the Committee on the Constitutional System and their well considered recommendations regarding constitutional and sub-constitutional reform. Although Lyndon Johnson, a liberal Democrat, and Ronald Reagan, a conservative Republican, amid a host of other political leaders including the centrist, recently defeated Democratic representative from South Carolina John Spratt, have endorsed the four year, presidential concurrent, term for the House of Representatives, the Democratic Party has never raised it as a public issue.

Let us remember, secondly, that the need for campaign finance reform is more pressing now than it has ever been, presidential and congressional candidates once again breaking contribution and spending records in the election of 2012. In spite of the many small internet contributions that went to President Obama, even his ostensibly left-of-center Democratic Party campaign continued to give only the most tepid lip service to the small "d" democratic necessity. Obama, as in 2008, rang up huge contributions from the people he should not be beholden to, particularly in the financial industries of banking, insurance, real estate, and the Wall Street investment houses that were so responsible for the bubble, and bubble-bursting, that thrust our country, and the rest of the world, into recession.

Further, let us not be buffaloed by those who argue that the biannual increases in spending on our political campaigns still amounts to only a few dollars per citizen. That's bad accounting. The figures that the campaigns report and the Federal Election Commission records are only the ante, the down payment. Any determination of the real cost of America's campaigns must include the tax breaks, the subsidies and the jobs taken overseas, as well as the costs of the lobbyists themselves, all of which are many times a multiple of the direct candidate contribution. The contributors wouldn't have made the investment if it wasn't going to pay off, and pay off it certainly has. In keeping with our purpose here, I ask only that we begin looking at the cognitive form of such large contributions, the analytic nature of that lobbyist-generated, unencumbered near-contract not only prostituting the will of the American people but slowing America's dialectical movement into the twenty-first century's global community along with it. I will discuss a third failure of America's parties, particularly the Democratic Party, regarding the issue of global parties in the next chapter.

So I merely repeat my call for the national adoption of a two and two-half, ideologically outriggered party system. Further, although I was not a proponent of proportional representation for a long time because I feared that coalition governments would only weaken the government vis à vis the private sector, I have reexamined that position in the face of the need to assure third and fourth party representation in our government. A coalition government with full representation for what a party such as the Greens believes cannot be more supine than a party that has surrendered so mercilessly to the interests. I also believe in both federally mandated, reasonable thresholds for third party ballot access, public funding for political campaigns, and the adoption of Instant Runoff Voting, whereby a voter can choose a preferred candidate and then have her vote shifted to a second candidate should her first choice not finish in the top two. These devices will provide a better range of perspectives within the American electoral process. They will also provide for the synthetically derived creations of policy determination that better ensure dialectical progress for our country regarding its global contradictions (specifically the unwillingness to sign human rights, women's rights, children's rights, criminal jurisdiction and a variety of other reasonable treaties) as we move along in this century's second decade.

The short of it is that the Democratic Party is nowhere near the party that should range from the center of the cognitive continuum to the reasonable perspectives that support a progressive but non-totalitarian left. Though it is not always appropriate to contrast the politics of America with Europe, it is worthwhile to note how infrequently the American Democratic Party includes individuals from the arts, or of a generally theoretical bent of mind, within their counsels. In the American Democratic Party, the Natural Left portion of the subjective, psychological, spectrum, from which the party should be drawing its most innovative thinkers, barely exists. Whereas in all intellectual fields we expect the best theoretical minds to be pushing the envelope of understanding through basic research (when you take your child to a doctor you expect the latest of *JAMA* and *New England Journal of Medicine* findings to be within your physician's grasp), not a single first tier theoretical mind exists in all of American politics. Even the late Democratic Senator from New York Daniel Patrick Moynihan, whom I greatly admired for his willingness to step outside the academy and who was expert in issues dealing with the African-American family, urban life, demographics, and who had the courage to vote against Bill Clinton's awful welfare reform bill in 1996, was not a theorist.

Ironically, the closest thing to an abstract mind, a sort of B-minus housing of a theoretical capability, exists within a member of the Republican Party with whom I substantively disagree on just about everything. It belongs to Newt Gingrich. Gingrich has some theoretical construct in his sometimes twisted mentality. In all the years I have listened to the Democrat Bill Clinton intone about politics, in contrast, I have heard nothing that approaches a robust abstraction. I once heard him explain how he thought history moved forward, insisting on the incremental nature of that process. Yes, some periods of history have evolved incrementally. The Dark Ages hardly evolved at all. But even the Darwinian biologists have settled on the quantum, or the "big leap" nature of biological adaptation in the species. Virtually all *major* historical changes in human history came in the dialectical form. Hegel understood that.

So, within the two and two half party model, a half party like the Greens may now be the best party to fill the void that is made available with the exclusion of the artistic and theoretical mind by the Democrats and the passing of the democratic socialists and co-op creators who were of the psychological left. The Greens are growing in several states, placing a member into the Arkansas state legislature in 2008, and again in 2012, and having a gubernatorial candidate in Illinois top 10% of the vote in 2006, as well as a courageous mayor, Gayle McLaughlin, who stands up to the banks on home foreclosures in Richmond, California. The Green Party may be the appropriate intellectual home for the artistically and theoretically minded, such dispositions more likely to stand for resistance to powerful economic interest groups and, not unlike the democratic socialists of two generations ago, standing as well for policies that benefit America's most challenged citizens. The Natural Left is available now, most strongly in the parties that lie at the intersection of Northeastern, Upper Midwestern, and West Coast left-of-center heritages, along with the emergence of a global party that proudly sports international figures like the late Vaclav Havel, Mikhail Gorbachev, the former German foreign minister Joschka Fischer, and the long-held Colombia hostage Ingrid Betancourt. That party is Die Grünen. But if not within the Greens, the mind that creates the Hegelian synthetic cognition in American and other nation's politics will eventually find a home. As for the right, I'll let them deal with how to accommodate the chasm that exists between their religious conservatives and the now aging University of Chicago economic purists. It's time for the right to be more splintered than the left anyway.

As I said at the outset, if I hope for one thing more than any other concerning the inclusion of the Natural Left in the real world of American politics, it is that it will act as a cross weave for so many objectively based left groupings that have always had a sufficient number of subjectively left personalities within them, all waiting to do what for them is only natural. With the inspiration that a new political self-consciousness can bring, the Natural Left can forge broader linkages on the left through the awakening of such personalities than American politics has ever achieved. Please do not forget the foundational notion here: *for every objectivity, there is a subjectivity.* I say again that in the twenty-first century, the most discriminated against citizen within both the American private and public sectors, regardless of her objective status, may now be the citizen whose mind is of the synthetic cognition. That mind is not fairly represented in a political system that has become nothing more than a collection of objective groups, and a corresponding collection of the analytic personalities that dominate the leadership of our public institutions over time, much as traditional organization theory has long demonstrated. Just as with the theoretical temperament, there is no one of the artistic temperament of a Havel, a Hašek, or a Bohumil Hrabal (*Closely Watched Trains*), in the American Democratic Party. For America, the contradiction at the second stage of the twenty-first century historical dialectic remains unanswered, principally because it has not yet been asked.

References

Robert B. Reich, *Beyond Outrage: Expanded Edition, What Has Gone Wrong With Our Economy and Our Democracy And How To Fix It*, New York, Knopf, 2012.

Buckley v. Valeo, 424 U. S. 1, (1976).

Citizens United v. F. E. C. 558 U. S. 08-208, (2010).

Chapter Fourteen

The World

Weaving the Natural Left's cognitions into the emerging global political order will be even more difficult than weaving Natural Left cognitions into our nation's politics. The placing of the Psychological or Natural Left into the theoretical dialogue, and then into the real world policies of international realities will, at a minimum, require purposeful, unashamedly ideological, activity.

Let us begin, as with Lincoln, by looking at where we are. The world, politically, is still far more a creature of the nation state than many expected it would be as credible global political institutions came into existence after World War II. I am a great admirer of the visionary scholar Richard A. Falk who, along with Saul H. Mendlovitz, Rajni Kathari, Ali Mazuri and other idealist thinkers, created what was called the World Order Models Project in the 1970s. That project's many fine publications challenged our thinking about the world's difficulties and urged the creation of the very global institutions that would transcend the conflicts of the nation-state system. I still believe in much of what those good people wrote. But for better or worse the nation state will be with us for a very long time, with even the laudable European trans-national experiment lurching forward in an irregular cadence. At least, however, there is a vision.

There is no question then that the world's institutions will and must increasingly impact the planet and its politics and we can confidently assign an ideological flavor to how various institutions impact the global mosaic. Currently, the United Nations knits the nation state in ways that respond to the peace, education, and welfare needs of the world. It does so in a manner that is not at all incompatible with the Natural Left. Clearly, some NGOs, or non-governmental organizations, minister admirably to the pressing health, education, and occupational needs of less developed populations. Significant religious figures like His Holiness the Dalai Lama, or South Africa's Reverend Desmond Tutu, have also attempted to contribute to a peaceful transcendence of conflicting national identifications. These figures, and their work, are clearly of the synthetic mind.

But just as clearly, global organizations like the International Monetary Fund, the World Bank, free trade zones, and other financially based institutions demonstrate the still gathering strength of the analytic cognitive form throughout the world, even in the context of their sometimes-sincere goal of assisting world wide economic development. Even more powerfully, the private, trans-national corporation is an almost wholly analytic entity. Some say that they are global governments unto themselves. At a minimum, the trans-national corporation, like most domestic corporations, marginalizes the development of the kind of global counterbalances that could and should be found in a cognitively balanced global regime.

What has escaped the attention of so many American political figures is the potential role of trans-national political parties in not only bringing peace and economic development to selected areas of the world, but in simultaneously bringing about the kind of twenty first century global order that does not permit the analytic form to dominate the new landscape. Here the European experience is instructive again. Europe's nation states developed new levels of trust after World War II as they built new institutions on the robustly synthetic vision of figures like Jean Monnet and Robert Schuman. A trans-European institution like the European Parliament might have been nothing more than a ceremonial meeting place for representatives of those nations, but it has proved to be more than that. It proved to be more than that because trans-national European political parties were part of the mix, with even conservative trans-national parties like the Christian Democrats but more significantly workers and human welfare parties like the Social Democrats assisting greatly in the integration of post-war Europe. The notion of a Mediterranean Union, advocated recently by the former French President Nicolas Sarkozy, is a synthetic step of potentially even greater importance, it seeking to bridge religious and cultural boundaries in a more dramatic way than the European Union. As I write, Croatia has become the European Union's twenty-eighth member. Latvia is poised to become the eighteenth member of the Euro Zone, with Lithuania to follow. These country's parties link with other European parties.

Let us not misunderstand. Parties are not inherently synthetic any more than nation states are inherently analytic. Roughly half of all the world's political parties are conservative, after all, largely doing the bidding of their nation's corporations. But, all things equal, the transcendence of parties beyond the nation state borders of Europe, even in the case of the more conservative parties, has enabled the progress of human rights, worker rights, environmental protections, and other encumbrances on the analytic, private contract to proceed more readily than they would have had national representatives, without trans-national party linkages, sat alone in places like the European Parliament, the European Commission, and the European Council. In these contexts, all political parties are at least partially synthetic.

To a lesser extent, I understand that transnational political parties in places like Latin America have been more than marginally helpful in quieting international rivalries on that continent. At the same time, they have assisted in the bringing about of a more prosperous and stable middle class within nation-states that had seemed, even well into the 1970s if not beyond, to be locked into political instability, economic inequity, and international hostility. As with Europe, the Latin American parties have not been exclusively synthetic, or of the Natural Left, in their orientations. But, in the overall, they have facilitated the kinds of discussions, not yet in a Latin American parliament to be sure, that has made the above economic, social, and most importantly political progress, possible.

What, then, of the United States? Why is it that the country that at least for a while longer will have the largest economy in the world, and at the same time has been for a long while the most prominent political and military state, has done nothing, absolutely nothing, to generate trans-national political parties? I don't have a ready answer to that question. But surely some of the answer lies in America's all too prominent sense of uniqueness, a failing that manifests itself in everything from not signing reasonable international treaties on human rights, children's rights, an international court, etc. to not lowering its flag at the opening and closing Olympic ceremonies. If you believe that globalization in the twenty-first century is as inevitable as the Industrial Revolution, or even the Neolithic Revolution, were in their times, I can only think that this process will benefit from a philosophical perspective that moves beyond objectively based philosophies. In a 1996 article published in *Alternatives*, a journal created by Richard Falk and his WOMP colleagues, one-time president of the International Studies Association Charles W. Kegley, Jr. and I called the creation of a global political party "the next step" to a global polity. It is passing strange, is it not, that American political parties have done little more than offer technical, that is phone bank, polling, and similar advice to overseas parties as well as send highly paid campaign industry specialists like Jim Carville to countries with which our government is strategically concerned?

The above American record, I submit, leans unrepentantly to the analytic cognitive side, since Republicans and their friends in the transnational corporations, of course, need the transnational party connection far less than those whom the Democrats purport to care about in their domestic and foreign agendas. I could not be more disappointed with the American Democratic Party that has not engaged in what the quantum but wholly natural development of global institutions requires in the twenty-first century, particularly in view of what other corners of the world have achieved. With the rest of the world calling, and with so many parts of the world, and even our immediate neighbor to the south, still enduring the drug gang related difficulties that they are, the single country status of the American Democratic Party stands out like a very sore thumb.

A final point on trans-national parties. In the run up to World War I, the Second International engaged in a determined effort to persuade the working classes within the combatant nations of Western Europe to resist being impressed into their nation's armies, thus hopefully proscribing the war. It didn't work. Nationalism triumphed over class identity, even with the long history of European wars and the involuntary induction of so many young men from the peasant and working classes. My own heritage grows out of more than one line of the impressed. It is my hope that the cross-weave of the subjectively identified global political party will fare far better at what would be its most admirable task. Hegel's Idealist progression, recall, built upon a gathering human consciousness. The same Jungian introspection that yields equitable representation for the cognitively synthetic personality should be able to manifest that representation in political parties that do what the objectively based identifications were not able to do nearly one hundred years ago. Beyond the equities of domestic politics, the peace of the world can be greatly advanced, I venture, by global political parties, one party consciously reflecting the Natural Left.

But there is a second issue that falls within the broad arena of global considerations. I am from Chicago and was raised with ethnic politics. Anyone from any of our country's major cities knows ethnic politics. I recall looking at the Illinois state budget when I was an undergraduate and finding, somewhere among the allocations for the Highway Department, The Education Department, and the Health Department, a line item allocation for Poland. That's right; the Illinois state government, for many years, gave money to the country Poland. That is ethnic politics.

It is perfectly understandable that in a nation of immigrants the identifications that new citizens have with their mother country, though now a foreign country, do not die. That identification may well continue through a second, or third, generation, or even longer. Of course, there are other causes of ethnic identification with foreign nations beyond coming from a country. Religious and ethnic identifications are real and, by themselves, they are wonderfully enriching things involving myth, culture, cuisine, and personal family histories that should never be casually abandoned.

But I offer two reflections on the issue of ethnic politics, the first suggesting a legally based framework for thinking about the various foreign country-based lobbies, and the second regarding the psychology of the foreign based lobby issue itself and the relationship of that psychology to a Natural Left theory. My view on these matters has evolved over the years.

In the common law of tort, or injury, there are three standards that span the spectrum from negligence to intentional harm. The first is called simple negligence. This is when someone injures someone else without meaning to, the finding of such fact by a judge or a jury invariably leading to what the law calls compensatory damages. The offender makes the victim whole, that is puts her back to *status quo ante*, or as close as possible to where she was before the injury.

The third, or most extreme, form of injury causation is when damage is intentionally inflicted. Someone wanted to cause harm, and the element of intentionality, or *scienter*, almost certainly requires what the law calls punitive damages. The offender is thus punished, not criminally but civilly, in a significant, more than restitutional way.

Between simple negligence and intentional harm, however, there is a middle category in the tort of personal injury. That middle category is called gross negligence, it describing a circumstance wherein the offender did not intentionally injure the victim but the injurer knowingly acted in such a manner that the law will say the offender should have anticipated that the conduct she was engaging in would cause injury. The injury, not intentional but not wholly accidental either since the act that caused the injury was intended, was what the law calls "foreseeable." A reasonable person would know that driving in a shopping mall parking lot at a high rate of speed might result in the striking of a child.

What I am suggesting is that foreign country-based lobbying within the United States, and as a nation of immigrants and religious believers we understandably have a lot of it, is capable of harm to our country in a way that is analogous to the middle level of negligent-to-intentional harm known as gross negligence. As the common law of agency holds, and as several religious writings speak to it including the Judeo-Christian scriptures, an individual cannot serve two masters. It is foreseeable, that is it is reasonable, that a person would realize that doing something for one master might not be in the best interest of the other.

For a very long time, I held to the view that the favor which many Americans had for foreign nations that had an ethnic, historical, or religious tie for them was cosmopolitan, or even integrative in ways that are similar to what I just argued regarding global political parties. This still might be true, in rare contexts. But it is clear to me now that it is not true in most contexts. I confess that I have been influenced recently by a rereading of the Farewell Address by the father of our country. George Washington penned that message in utter frustration nearly a year before leaving office in 1797, complaining about how a "passionate attachment" to a foreign country, which so frequently led to exercising a political favor for that country, was harmful to our nation. By that time, Washington had had more than enough of the long-running Jefferson-Hamilton, Francophile-Anglophile disputes that had dogged his entire presidency.

I also confess that my increasingly frustrated feeling about foreign country lobbies has been influenced by the reality of the leverage that such lobbies have recently exerted on our government. That leverage, at a minimum, has raised the foreseeable risk, if it has not already created the reality, that our country will be harmed by the favor given to a foreign country, along with the fact that our most challenged citizens will pay a disproportionate share of the price of actions like the military adventures outside our borders that foreign country lobbies have too frequently urged.

Most of the forty-five hundred soldiers and marines killed in the Iraqi War were from lower-middle to economically marginal American families. Many were not American citizens. These brave and trusting men and women were sacrificed in at least some part by a policy that was supported by Israeli, and sometimes British, foreign nation interests in our country, as well as by Iraqi interests that feigned friendship with the United States in order to encourage military adventurism in their favor. It goes almost without saying that the influence of Arab/Muslim nations like Saudi Arabia, whose royal family had the run of the White House in the George H. W. Bush administration, is also wholly outsized, girded of course by our nation's long time dependence on its oil, and this in spite of the Saudi's housing of more terrorists that plot against our country than any other Arab/Muslim country.

I recognize that the above condemnation of foreign country lobbies has historically possessed the color of conservative rather than left of center politics. It was often seen as nativistic, and maybe it was on occasion, if it is evaluated solely from the perspective of an objective, pre-sub-atomic understanding. But from the perspective of a sub-atomic political model, I submit that the nationalistic orientations of lobbies that attempt to leverage the American government on behalf of their "passionate attachment" finds them to be anything but of the Natural Left. In fact, it is they who are the conservatives, their wish for unencumbered access to our country's policy making being little different from the wish for unencumbered access by the corporations.

Perhaps counter-intuitively, the Natural Left is represented by those who stand for an American foreign policy that simply maintains the primacy of our national interest, and that is in the best interest of all American citizens and particularly those who are the most likely to bear the burden of war. The Natural Left, again, insists on a perspective that looks beyond the regions and religions of the world that somehow cannot seem to find, if indeed they always want, peace. The Natural Left would set our country's direction on a better path for finding peace by responding to our most generous national instincts, and not the selfish instincts of warring foreign countries and their all too vocal supporters here. Americans should never forget that it was the British who finagled us into World War I, a war that we should never have participated in. It was the British, with the French, who reinforced Woodrow Wilson's support for outrageous reparations against Germany after the war, in spite of Wilson's proclamations about an armistice without victory and a peace without reparations. But of course it all comes around. The British and Lloyd George's desire to "squeeze them [the Germans] until the pips squeak," once supported by the ostensibly idealistic Wilson, wrote the first paragraph of an aspiring German politician's stock speech, assuring another tragic war as well as the tragedy of the Holocaust.

In short, there is nothing nationalistic, or chauvinistic, about the position that identifies and opposes foreign country lobbies when they foster an American foreign policy that is not in our country's interest. I have chastised the American Democratic Party for not creating transnational, or global, political alliances. I have called it a single country party as we aspire to a political coming together of the world that is reasonably balanced between the analytic and the synthetic cognitions, aided by a global party, maybe the Greens. That balance, I believe, ensures equity across the entire range of issues, at the same time that it is our best response to the nationalistic exhortations of those foreign country lobbies who advocate violent action in favor of their favored nation-state, whether it's the Armenian lobby, the Cuban lobby, the Arab or Israeli lobbies, or the lobby that so few dare speak its name though it has gotten our country into far more trouble than any other: the British lobby.

Beyond World War I, let us not forget that the British initiated the current Middle Eastern carnage with their arbitrary drawing of national borders in 1920, their crushing of a justified Palestinian revolt in the late 1930s, their bombing of the Jews in 1946 (I went to graduate school with a Lancaster pilot who confessed shame at being part of the Jewish bombing), the wheedling of Allen and John Foster Dulles, and subsequently Eisenhower, into the now admitted overthrowing of the Iranian premier Mosadegh in 1953 (after Truman turned Churchill down the year before, and a dear colleague of mine's father being tortured by the Shah's secret police after serving in the Mosadegh cabinet), the ill-advised invasion of the Suez Canal with the French and Israelis in 1956, capped off by Tony Blair's support for the Iraqi War based upon a laughable notion of an alleged WMD's range. One point, to be sure, for the back benchers' saying "no" to the recent American Syrian foray.

Nothing against the average bloke, please understand, or those whom Lord Devlin called the "man on the Clapham Omnibus," but when the Canadians, the French, the Germans, and so many others of our real friends said "no" to Bush II, Dick Cheney, Donald Rumsfeld, and the neo-cons Paul Wolfowitz, Richard Perle, Douglas Feith, David Frum, Norman and John Podhoretz, Jeanne Kilpatrick, and Bill Kristol, it was the Eton-Sandhurst-Oxford crowd that cowardly said "yes." The Senate having rejected the brave exhortation of Michigan Senator Carl Levin's plea to send the matter to the UN Security council, it was the British who unlatched the last barrier to the catastrophe that continues in Iraq today.

None of the foregoing would have happened if it had not been for the machinations of a lobby that surpasses even the Israeli lobby in American political influence. This reality becomes rain puddle clear when the full triad of pro-American choices, anti-American choices, and that middle classification of non-American choices, like the middle category of gross negligence in the common law triad of liability, is laid before us. Non-American choices, generated from non-American passionate attachments and the willingness of the adherents of those choices to target susceptible members of Congress for a long time, while at the same time contributing inordinate sums to political candidates and political parties who opposed them, destined our country to unfortunate foreign policy choices. The cost of these choices was wholly foreseeable, for those who wished to see them.

A final word on foreign country lobbies. Yes, I know what allies, and alliances, are. But allies are not partners, and alliances are not partnerships. A partnership is an equal relationship, whether in a marriage, a small business, or in any other cooperative arrangement where the burdens and rewards are equally shared. No political alliance with a foreign country is a partnership, although some diplomats carelessly use that term when the flags are neatly pleated in rows behind the two sets of hands that envelop their respective podiums. The American office holder's constitutional obligation to our citizenry, hopefully including that cognitively balanced integration into a global system because that form of synthetically generated integration is in our country's best interest, outweighs any contractually negotiated, analytically formed, and most importantly influence-based alliance with a foreign country. Those American citizens who advocate favored treatment for any foreign country, beyond the express obligations of a treaty, knowingly import foreseeable harm to our country.

America's principal founder understood that this kind of thing could happen. The common law understood that it could happen, and the Drafter of the Decalogue understood something every bit as profound. We should be true to our alliance obligations, of course, but only until the stretching of those obligations harms America, as it surely does when Israel continues to build West Bank settlements and neither Big Box party has the courage to stop them. Without a whit of sympathy for the Arab governments that harbor terrorists, enflame anti-Semitism, and all too often use the plight of the Palestinians as an excuse not to make sincere overtures to the nation that has every right to exist without bombings, assassinations, and the fear of same; and without the romantic attachment that so many of the objective left cling to regarding irresponsible leaders like Yasser Arafat, who refused to respond to the good faith Ehud Barak/Bill Clinton offer regarding ninety-seven percent of the West Bank, I commend the former Republican President George H. W. Bush and his able Secretary of State James A. Baker for their withholding of loan guarantees when Israel refused to stop building settlements. They did the right thing, for our country. And let us not forget that Bill Clinton's otherwise laudable eighth-year peace effort was made far more difficult because of his prior seven years of something that came nowhere near what the distinguished former Illinois Republican Senator Charles H. Percy, whom I knew and thought highly of, called "even-handedness." The lobby didn't want even-handedness and it disposed of Senator Percy.

References

Richard A. Falk, *A Study Of Future Worlds*, New York, The Free Press, 1975.

William P. Kreml and Charles W. Kegley, Jr., "A Global Political Party: The Next Step," *Alternatives*, June, 1996, 123–134.

Saul H. Mendlovitz, *On The Creation Of A Just World Order*, New York, The Free Press, 1975.

Chapter Fifteen

Religion

In this final chapter before the epilogue I will address something that many argue is too often missing from the perspective of the political left. It is religion. The critics are right. The vision of the traditional left, even with its admirable humanism and its insistence on the political equality of all men and women, along with its respect for the world around us (including the other creatures of the world and the environment we all live in) does not sufficiently explain the world. Neither does it sufficiently inspire the kind of secular political activity that is necessary to achieve subatomic equity. What follows is my paean to the "bounded" relativity (as opposed to the random relativity) of religious perspective, from the orthodoxies that mark the traditional religions on one hand to the humanistic, conceptually horizontal religions that include secularism and the agnostic viewpoint on the other. Too many atheists, I'm afraid, are part of the ideological curl back of the objective variable, with a Stalin-like rigidity to boot. I am a Taoist, a religion that at one and the same time is a creed with certain beliefs, but also a creed with a kind of built-in discomfort about too much belief. The Way that can be spoken is not the Way.

I think the best format for describing the relativity of religious perspectives, within the context of a political philosophy of the Natural Left, is to portray a pattern of a history, specifically a history of how the Western religions evolved in a manner that demonstrates the emergence of the psychological range. I believe there have been seven identifiable stages of Western religious history, with Stages I and VII having both interesting parallels and an instructive contrast. Using the metaphor of the clock, I would describe the seven stages as:

Stage I: In pagan times, religion richly intertwined the supernatural and the natural. There was a psychological balance within these beliefs. The sense of authority that the universe held for pagans was balanced by a sense of human involvement and the organic wholeness of the universe. Members of a pagan community generally held to this form, the single belief system of a pagan people allowing sufficient range within it to satisfy the sum of the psychological orientations within the population. Individual members could comfortably lean towards one orientation or the other. Six o'-clock.

Stage II: The stage of polytheism, particularly of the Greek and Roman variety, witnessed the emergence of more authoritarian godhead figures. Supernatural authority began to dominate natural authority, although the two remained linked by the jurisdictional nature of the authoritarian figures. Gods were identified with localities, such as Athens and Rome, as well as with various aspects of life such as war, love, medicine, music, etc. Eight o'clock.

Stage III: Though pre-classical in its origin, Constantine's acceptance of the monotheistic, Christian God required an even more authoritarian view of the universe. God is now the Creator, Lawgiver, and Enforcer of His Law rolled into one. The supernatural even more clearly dominates the natural, the analytically well defined, authoritarian relationship of a Supreme Being with each subject is increasingly unchallenged. Unanimity is enforced by the Commandments. Secular authority falls into line. Ten o'clock.

Stage IV: High Christendom, after the exclusion of the Gnostic and the acceptance of the Pauline and Nicene orthodoxies, marks the pinnacle of the authoritarian position. A supernatural descendant of the Deity, the Nicene determination of the liturgical creed, and the Augustinian obsession with guilt and redemption triumph over the early Christian, Oriental, and humanistic perspective of Jesus and the original gospels. Twelve o'clock.

Stage V: The Middle Ages to the Renaissance was a period of formal Christian dominance, although a degree of synthetic deviation grows out of a disaffection with an increasingly corrupt and authoritarian Church and the temporal Empire whose allegiance it claimed. Islam had removed the supernatural human character, already non-existent in Judaism. Reaction to the Inquisitions of the late Middle Ages scarred the Church, while the Renaissance confirmed the compromise of faith with reason in Thomas Aquinas's *Summa Theologica* in a way that supplanted the purely faith-based orientation of Duns Scotus and the Franciscans. The growth of the Humanist perspective in Italy, including Petrarch along with the paintings of Giotto, and the writings of the Dutch Erasmus and the acceptance of religious pluralism by figures such as the English Thomas More, marked the acceptance of at least a measure of doctrinal differentiation. Martin Luther's Reformation and John Calvin's Presbyterianism, even with the subjection of the Czech Hussites, assured religious pluralism. Two o'clock.

Stage VI: The Age of Reason and the Enlightenment signaled the acceptance of openly deistic beliefs such as Voltaire's "watchmaker" notion of the Creator and His Creation. The Reformation's acceptance of left-wing sects such as the Anabaptists marked the rejection of authoritarian Christianity by some and a revival of a more naturalistic perspective on the earth, its inhabitants, and a variety of ways to relate to the Deity. The dispersion of Protestant faiths, from Unitarianism to Methodism, increasingly mirrored the differentiations of human personalities and their varied proclivities for authoritarian-to-non-authoritarian visions of the universe. Four o'clock.

Stage VII: Modernity and the contemporary world witnessed the dispersions described above as they reached across the psychological range. Marking the authoritarian to the anti-authoritarian, the cognitively analytic to cognitively synthetic spectrum, this range was tolerated within much of the Western world. Even newer faiths, such as Baha'i, emphasized an ecumenical perspective on religion and the role of a succession of prophets from religions running to the nineteenth century Bah'ha'ulah. The Dead Sea Scrolls and the Nag Hammadi manuscripts, whether the latter are Gnostic or not, revived legitimate claims of Old Testament reinterpretation and Gnostic Christianity respectively. Secularism flourishes. Six o'clock.

As you can tell, Stage VII partially mirrors the original, Stage I, position, each encompassing a full range of psychologies. But the difference is that the range of psychologies now manifests itself *across* the spectrum of religions and secular beliefs rather than *within* any single belief. In short, virtually all traditional Western beliefs have suffered some fracture, largely because their original, "vertical" teachings did not well represent the naturally non-authoritarian preference for "horizontal" ethical positions, ranging from a cognitively synthetic religious ecumenicism to a Western interest in Asian religions, as well as humanism and secularism.

Though many religious liberals still retain membership in traditional, more or less "vertical" religions, long-standing internal conflicts within those religions, along with the continuing religious and secular struggle within the Abrahamic religious family generally, have contributed to the loss of membership and the shifting of some of these orthodox religions towards ever-greater fundamentalism. Do not forget that even mainstream Christian religions sustain missionary efforts that are perceived as threatening to Muslim and Jewish adherents, thus causing great conflict. Some evangelical Christian seminaries teach the "stealth missionary" technique, whereby the proselytizer does not reveal her true identity while embedding within the targeted population as a health worker, teacher, or the like, waiting for the opportunity to convert vulnerable populations, frequently orphans of war that the American Army has been involved in. The general American public knows little about this, although stealth missionary work is one of the principal sources for the fear of Christianity in the Muslim world. Muslims, of course, also engage in vigorous missionary activity, particularly across sub-Saharan Africa, and their efforts have too often been accompanied by horrid political and economic subjugations, such as what went on in the Sudan for far too long.

In sum, by the beginning of the twenty-first century, the classical cognitive differentiation between the analytic and synthetic forms had worked its way through the entire religious spectrum, perhaps somewhat more fully in the non-Islamic West although the recent conflict within Egypt evidences the religious/secular divide, just as it had within the philosophical and jurisprudential spectrums that we reviewed earlier. The cognitive differentiation is that powerful. I believe that the religious range, perhaps even more strongly than the intellectual ranges that evidenced the work-

ing out of the cognitive fissions and fusions in various intellectual
fields that I reviewed earlier, further grounds the cognitive spectrum as the core of a sub-atomic, dialectically Idealist, philosophical perspective. The religious range, by its very acknowledgment
as a spectrum in the minds of increasing numbers of fair-minded
people, should but strengthen the belief in the cognitively understood ideological range and the embracing of that range as the key
to sub-atomic political equity. Perhaps this is the place to begin to
address Barbara Ehrenreich's and Susan Cain's notions of psychological bias, now within a public rather than private venue, and
begin to address the bias of temperament in American politics.

A final matter. I have had no formal architectural training whatever, but as a boy I spent a good deal of time in the studio of the
architect Barry Byrne, one of the five principal protégés of Frank
Lloyd Wright in his Oak Park studio. His son, Patrick Barry, and
I were good friends. I remember with much delight watching Mr.
Byrne sit atop his high stool before his drafting table, and I particularly loved watching the construction of detailed models for the
churches and residences that he worked on. This gentle man was
always generous with his time, explaining how he did what he did
and giving me much of the appreciation for architecture that has
lasted throughout my lifetime. Being from Chicago, I also learned
to appreciate architecture outside any office, and as I walked among
the varied fingers in the sky, Chicago being the sole American city
whose architecture represents all architectural periods, I dreamed
of designing one interesting building, just one, before I shuffled
off.

Life takes funny turns, frequently postponing youthful aspirations
until a much later time. In the fall of 1994, and again in the fall of
1997, I was a visiting professor at the University of Peking in Bei-
jing, China. It was there that I began to tinker with a building design based upon the Taoist notion of the yin-yang. With the help
of a wonderful draftsperson, Pamela J. Gleaton, and then with the
skill of a most creative architect, J. Temple Ligon, I have now completed the penultimate plans for a unique home, one built on the
ancient Taoist symbol. The plans are below and I give them to you.

The principle ordering of these plans is based on a comple-
mentarity of opposites that is at the core of the yin-yang. As you
can see, there is one large yin-yang design, separating the couplet
of bedrooms and the kitchen from the third bedroom and the liv-
ing/dining room. But there are also second, smaller, yin-yang sep-
arations, that being within the two bedroom circle and the other
side. If someone would like to put French doors between the bedrooms, it might be interesting. Also, if someone would like more
openness between the living/dining room and the third bedroom,
the wall at the center could be shortened, or removed all together.
I prefer having the wall go half way myself, permitting a movable
screen to mostly enclose the third bedroom area but having it available for entertaining. Fireplaces should be placed at both axes.

But, again, the meaning of the design is clear. The unification
of space that is represented by the full circle, and the integration of
the sub-units that is accentuated by the two foyers and by the placement of the doors, is intended to represent the essential Taoist notion that what at first appears to be a contradiction is in fact only
part of a larger whole. The architectural opposites are indeed complementary, all part of a richer unity, the differentiation ironically
providing for the omissions within each side.

If you decide to build this home, first decide on what diameter
you wish it to have. The draft I present here is for a diameter of fifty-
five feet, giving you roughly 2300 round feet. You must do the
final stage yourself, plugging in the wiring, plumbing, heating and
cooling, roofing, etc. into the plans, however you want them, and
with your architect. Please use green materials as much as possible, including panels. I have been assured that with a fifty foot or
larger diameter, the gyp board will bend sufficiently to permit easy
construction. There is a new hemp board that comes from England.
It is better environmentally than the old gyp board, as it absorbs
moisture.

The studs, in any case, will have to be closer together than they
need to be in a flat wall. If you wish to use mesh and old-fashioned
plaster, which is always nicer than gyp board, there are still arti-
sans in the Latino community who do that sort of work. I suppose
I could have sold these plans, on which I do possess a copyright. But

I have decided that if I gave them away, they would, in the Taoist way, become even more valuable. I ask only that you inform me of the progress of your home as you get roughly halfway along in its construction. Contact me at the Department of Political Science, University of South Carolina, Columbia, SC, 29208, USA, and I will get back to you. All the best, both to you and your new home. All the best as well to what I hope are your new political insights, they, as you have already discerned, being not unrelated to the design of the home.

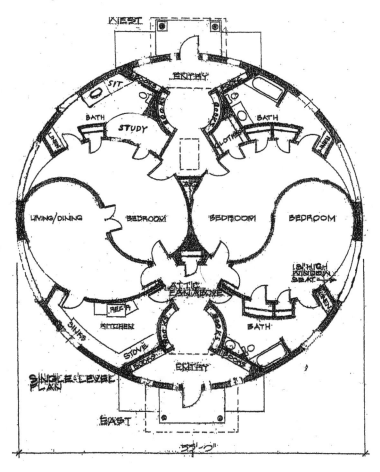

Epilogue

In 2008, an important election was held and the candidate who needed to win, Senator Barrack Obama of Illinois, did. Although this was the Senator who sat grinning next to the other Senator who had just lied about the Levin amendment that would have postponed and possibly prevented the Iraqi War, Senator Obama was still preferable to the aging Republican candidate who, with his choice for vice president (even worse than Obama's) and for other reasons, might have done serious harm to our country. Though I am a Green, and though I voted for the Green candidate in a non-competitive state, I am enough of a *realo* rather than a *fundi*, to use the German Green terms, to think of a political outcomes' impact upon the average, and particularly the most challenged of American citizens, apart from the impact that outcome may have on my party. The McCain/Palin duo, along with the people who would have served in their administration, along with the possibility of the succession to the presidency of Palin, was too scary to contemplate.

This writing finds the Obama administration fully into its second term, enmeshed in difficulties that it seems only partly capable of resolving. Although I have no substantial complaint about most of Obama's appointments, I must note an almost reassuring touch of old-fashioned bigotry in the Obama administration. The president's Secretary of the Navy and the Marines, the former Mississippi governor Ray Mabus, once responded to an inquiry, after we had amicably served together on a Newport Institute panel in Rhode Island, saying that I should buy a vowel for my last name. Why would any president, much less a gentleman of color, appoint a bigot like Ray Mabus to the position of Secretary of the Navy?

The fact is that it was Obama alone who moved me to add an epilogue to this book. He inspired me with how he closed one of the cabinet introduction ceremonies, the president-elect bragging on himself by saying he was doing such a wonderful job of bringing diversity into the government. Why would anyone think that the full inclusion of objective groups, like African-Americans, women, Latinos, Asians, etc., ensures the inclusion of the full range of humanity? The answer is because what he claimed was a long way from being sub-atomic.

The executive branch is every bit as devoid of the cognitive range from the center to where the objective spectrum bends back to the right as, say, Bill Clinton's and other recent Democratic cabinets have been. What is it about Democratic Party office holders that even an individual who wrote two sensitive, at moments introspective, books and who exquisitely spoke to the Trayvon Martin affair, still discriminates when it comes to the exclusion of those of theoretical, or artistic, temperament?

Sure, our country needs continued attention to discrimination against objective groups, even as the election of this African-American president represents a significant achievement. The November, 2008 election of a Vietnamese member of Congress, in the same state where an Indian-American already sat as governor, along with the election of an Indian-American governor in South Carolina in 2012, speaks well for our nation's improving objective diversity in politics. But for all the promise of change, this president now presides in the Oval office, like so many of his predecessors, with essentially like-minded advisers. Did the professor who once taught at the University of Chicago Law School not learn the lesson from physics that makes the sculpture just north of the corner of 57th and Ellis Street so important? This is where Enrico Fermi sustained the first nuclear reaction, in 1942, based on the sub-atomic breakthrough in physics. Professor, now president, Obama's home is just off 51st Street, between Greenwood and Ellis. The law school is on 60th Street, the nearest cross street being Ellis. I hatched the notion of a sub-atomic political theory, and scratched out the deeper meaning of *Shelley v. Kraemer*, at that sculpture. What grew out of what this sculpture represented was not all bad after all.

Simply put, Prof. Barrack Obama taught the Supreme Court's most important theoretical case wrong, but I would go easy on him because he was mistaught the case himself on the banks of the Charles. To be fair, he is no more afflicted than any other common law lawyer with the notion that a case means only what arguing lawyers and an opinion writing judge says it means. It's not true. Never has been. And, theory aside, has Obama not now witnessed how much America's ersatz party of the left half of the spectrum is different from the great bulk of left-of-center parties within the world's democracies by excluding the temperaments of the artist and the theorist, and getting a constitutional case like *Shelley v. Kraemer* wrong because the American lawyer cannot throw off the common law's methodology?

For the record, I like Vaclav Havel's drama, and Havel, remember, considered himself to be a Green. Again, the former Russian President Mikhail Gorbachev considers himself to be a Green, as does the long-time Colombian captive Ingrid Betancourt, and other leading world figures. I also like what former Secretary of State Madeleine Albright said about Czechoslovakia's first president, Thomas Masaryk, named on the monument at the U. of C.'s Wenceslas Square replica, on the ninetieth anniversary (2008) of the Czech national founding. Secretary Albright aptly noted that Masaryk was a philosopher who once taught near where this beautiful memorial rests, at the east end of the Plaisance, between 59th and 60th Streets. I have a particular fondness for the University of Chicago, and maintain a membership in its library society, in part because my grandmother was offered an art scholarship at the University shortly after its 1890 opening. Sadly, she was not permitted to go by her German father. Küche, Kirche, Kinder. My parents confirmed what I felt as a child. My temperament is much like hers. I have her paintings.

No, I do not ask for a politics, or a Supreme Court, that is dominated by theorists. Two hours in a philosophy panel at an occasional political science convention is pretty much all I can stand myself and the last thing this troubled nation needs is rococo ideological disputes and baroque doctrinaire solutions to our problems. But America's politics, maybe more than at any time since the Civil War, does require the full range of cognitive perspectives. We need, as Lincoln put it, "to think anew", and specifically to include the kind of mind that reflects the cognitive forms of Hegel's "Idea of Cognition" chapter in the Science of Logic, the mind that understands what *Shelley v. Kraemer* really stands for. Only the full participation of that kind of mind ensures equity in the day-to-day affairs of law and government, as well as the successful transcendence of the second, contradictory stage of the twenty-first century's historical dialect. Surely, this president must be aware of Lincoln's above dissembling: "I have not a fine education; I am not capable of entering into a disquisition on dialectics...."

Parties and the Dialectic

So what, then, of the Democratic Party, the party that would have us believe it represents the non-totalitarian left of center position in our nation's politics? If one looks solely at the differentiation between the substantive positions of various Democratic office holders and the sub-constitutional structural arrangements these office holders either created or ratified, that being at one level up the ladder of abstraction, what does one find? Yes, though President Jimmy Carter made earnest efforts to cool the damaging inflation of the late 1970s, and though he surely engaged in a beneficent foreign policy with advances in Latin American human rights, the Panama Canal Treaty, and, most importantly, the Camp David Accords between Egypt and Israel, the thirty-ninth president's obsession with detail, his inability to delegate, and, most damagingly, his inability to build bridges to even the Democratic majorities in Congress, all evidenced his analytic mind. There was never much of a synthesis to domestic policy under Jimmy Carter, was there?

I should also relate that if someone had tapped me on the shoulder at my 1965 law school graduation, whispering that in thirteen years my senior seminar paper on the Civil Aeronautics Board would be but scraps of paper, I would have chuckled. But that's exactly what happened; Jimmy Carter deregulated the airline industry in

1978. Ronald Reagan did not begin deregulation. A Democratic president did.

Similarly, Bill Clinton's laudable 1993 tax reform, along with initiatives like the earned income tax credit, surely manifested far more equitable priorities than the tax code revisions of Ronald Reagan in 1981, not to mention those of George H. W. Bush in 2001. But at the next level of abstraction again, the level where the structures of the mind meet the structures of government, where was President Clinton? If someone had told me that Clinton's revenue priorities would be accompanied by deregulations like that contained in the Telecommunications Act of 1996, allowing a further, Rupert Murdoch-benefiting concentration in the public's media or, worse, by the banking and financial services "Modernization Act" of 1999 that let loose the hedge funds, along with the earlier destruction of Glass-Steagall that had separated banking and investment, and finally the reappointment of the Ayn Rand acolyte Alan "something was missing in the model" Greenspan to head the Federal Reserve Board, I would not have chuckled. I would have been, and I still am, furious. When huge capital surpluses began to appear because of America's perpetual trade imbalances, thus accelerating the repatriation of American dollars that artificially drove down interest rates, Clinton-initiated deregulation permitted that money to foster the kind of lending, and eventual securitization of debt instruments, that led to the housing valuation bubble which, in turn, burst and caused the Global Recession. Clinton turned out to be a bank lover.

And what about free trade, the issue that perhaps more clearly than any manifests what kind of mind you have? Are you a Clay or a Calhoun? Well, everyone should be for free trade, when all things are equal, except that they never are. In the real, still mercantilist, world where every country protects their national interest, and even more importantly where our own corporations have shown no loyalty to our country and have shipped their jobs offshore, it's far more complex than that. When I was a visiting professor at the University of Peking in China in 1994, and again in 1997, I interviewed many citizens, on and off the campus. The Chinese, it was clear by 1997 if not before, were out to beat us. I have studied from afar the Russians, the Japanese, and, yes, even our European friends, all of whom protect and promote their industries vigorously, and I come to a simple conclusion. Of course, we should never go back to Smoot-Hawley and rank protectionism, but to callously shave the synthetic variable of American workers' jobs from the economic calculus in industry after industry has been terribly harmful to our country and, of course, the workers themselves. Most recently, we have Obama's secretly negotiated Trans Pacific Partnership initiative, which does little to protect the American worker who is so often not able to find new employment, or at best must reenter employment at a substantially lower salary, once she is laid off. What, too, of the investment capital taken off shore by the corporations? Thanks to Clinton, it was "check the box" in the tax code and the write-off for foreign taxes appeared, another product of a mediocre abstract mind.

Finally, what of anti-trust enforcement under President Clinton? Well, until the computer users of America screamed bloody murder over Microsoft's anti-competitive practices towards Netscape, Clinton's record was a sorry one indeed. A pedestrian belief in the self-regulatory calculus of competition, which was debunked by none other than Adam Smith in his writings about combinations in 1776, and debunked in the real world by Theodore Roosevelt's and W. H Taft's courageous enforcement of the moribund Sherman Anti-Trust Act in the early twentieth century, further evidence Bill Clinton's kind of mind.

Within the Congress, the record of Democratic office holders has been no better. It was the Democrat Joe Lieberman of Connecticut who held off SEC chair Arthur Levitt's wish to take a good look at the insurance industry, and particularly into companies like AIG, in 1999. The Democrats rewarded Lieberman with their vice-presidential nomination one year later, Lieberman returning the favor by endorsing George Bush in 2004. It was the Democratic Senator and former Democratic Party co-chair Chris Dodd of Connecticut who took the VIP Countrywide Financial mortgage with the "Friend of Angelo" (Mozilo) tag on it, and looked not at all at the outrages of home financing, though he was the ranking Democrat on the Senate Banking Committee. And it was New York Democrat Charles Schumer who would not let anyone, that is no one, get anywhere near *his* Wall Street with its debt swaps, its securitization of mortgages, its transparent Ponzi schemes that went on for years, along with the executive bonuses. These public servants not only did not extinguish the smoldering evidences of speculation and greed; their protection of unregulated industries threw gasoline on the fire. At this writing, Senator Schumer is fighting to delay the application of the "swaps rule" in commodities trading, which figures like Senator Elizabeth Warren (D-MA) understand is the key to reining in hedge fund excesses. But the Elizabeth Warrens are too rare in the Democratic Party, Assistant Senate Majority Leader Dick Durbin (D-IL) expressing his frustration with fellow Democrats who abandoned him on bank reform in 2009 by saying that the banks "frankly own the place." No, let's not let the Republicans off the hook. It was Jim Leach (R-IA) who fostered interstate banking, trusting Japanese bank asset figures that vastly overvalued their real estate holdings. But the Party of Jefferson and Jackson used to respond to these things. Now it doesn't.

So even allowing for the atrocious mismanagement of the Republican budgets under Ronald Reagan and George W. Bush (and recall that in the tax votes, the war votes, and in the unconscionable assaults on the Constitution like the Patriot Act and NDAA, the Democrats all too often went along), is there any wonder that the relative position of the United States vis à vis the rest of the world suffered its worst-ever decline in the period from roughly the middle of the 1970s to perhaps but two or three years ago? Is there any wonder that the national debt now stands at nearly seventeen trillion dollars, and until recently grew more rapidly than in any peacetime period, or that the wealth and income distributions within our population approach that of the Gilded Age? I am not surprised, and no one else should be. Cognitive structures of the mind, and the real world political structures that they utilize and too often further imbalance, lie above substantive policy positions on the ladder of abstraction. They are, again, more immediately responsive to cognitive preferences, such preferences having traditionally altered the unwritten, constitutionally flexible structures and processes of the American government. Somewhere in the late 1960s and early 1970s, much under the influence of counter-productive New Left thinking as I noted above, the party that once created and utilized strong public sector institutions in order to oppose rapacious private interests lost sight of its history, lost sight of its purpose, and lost sight of its implicit obligation to the synthetic cognition. Remember that a mere comparison of the record of one party to another party is the least sophisticated way to evaluate performance over time. It is the comparison of what a party has done with what that party promises to do that is the more sophisticated test. The Democrats, ostensibly the protector of the average citizen, in the contemporary position of the anti-federalists' protectors of the Constitution-era debtor, now fail that test.

The First Suggestion — Education

So what is to be done? It is fair, after all, to ask that question of any theorist and it is incumbent on any theorist to pause from the building of the mental model and suggest solutions to the world's real problems. And so I offer three suggestions, one dealing with education, one dealing with necessary changes in the American political system, and the third dealing with the creation of synthetically based institutions on a global scale, specifically the creation of a truly global political party. Let's begin with education.

With English Composition as my college minor field many years ago, I repair to the arts. Of course, a great deal of literature was required of all English students. But there was one option in the English Department that balanced a reading of the great works with a bit of performance. The composition sub-field choice was not selected by many of my fellow students, but I chose it. After the standard Literature and Composition freshman course, I had to take a nasty little offering on punctuation, grammar, etc. and then went on to three quarters of pure writing. The first course was poetry, the second short stories, with the third requiring everyone to write a novella. I loved it.

As I have grown older and as I have come to reunite with several people whom I knew when we were both much younger, I am struck by how many of those whom I had considered to be so creative, and in some cases even abstract in their thinking, who seem now to have lost all of that. Something died. What if we as a country decided that we should encourage more citizens to continue to develop their creative and abstract thinking talents throughout their adult years? What if all liberal arts colleges required that their students undertake at least a one year's course of actual performance in one of the arts? The inclusion of creativity within a good liberal arts curriculum is hardly a new idea. Good schools, like Sarah Lawrence, already offer it as a major part of a liberal arts option. Of course, liberal arts students should continue to read Shakespeare, observe Rembrandt, and listen to Beethoven. And let us concede that very few students will ever come close to achieving what those creative giants did. But what if our best students, and liberal arts students are still our best students, began the practice of writing, or painting, or composing, or sculpting, or designing architecture, in a way that encouraged them to continue to at least be able to think like one who does this, throughout their lives? Might not this one pedagogical innovation have a wonderful impact, over time, on the cognitive imbalances of American politics? Didn't Bill Clinton rush out to drink beer with Havel and Hrabal when he first visited Prague? He did, but he never put people of such temperaments in his cabinet or inner circle. His political club was dominated by people like the small minded pollster Dick Morris and the "self regulation" sycophants he collected from Wall Street and the banks.

And, finally, what if one, just one, political theory class completed the canon of Locke, Hobbes, Mill, Rousseau and so on by letting students write their own political philosophy? You never know what they might create, both in theory and, maybe, in the world of real politics.

Secondly, let me suggest something regarding our legal education that may assist in the rebalancing of our government, particularly in view of the fact that so many of America's political figures have legal backgrounds. Some citizens complain about the predominant number of lawyers in government. I differ. The law provides a sound foundation for a public career. The problem is that

virtually all American legally-educated political figures have an English common law education, an education that, as above, has its
strengths and its weaknesses, I surviving three years at Northwestern Law School myself.

For openers, why is it that so little of the Anglo-American legal
discussion includes the sub-texts of cases, beyond what the written
opinion speaks to? The framework for a legal decision in the Anglo-
American world is largely set by the lawyers, each working with the
incentive of narrowing the field of inquiry to the relevant legal
precedent that brings victory to their side of the argument. This is
hardly a formula for theoretical rumination.

To be sure, the English common law carries a great flexibility to
it, the case method allowing for adaptations of precedents in ways
that may, at least in some cases, facilitate the finding of justice in
the present case where a more structured reading might not. There
is also a welcome stability to what amounts to a double strutted
political and legal arrangement within an English common law nation. The law's relatively greater independence from government
vis à vis continental legal systems permits the law to keep an eye
on government in ways that more intertwined systems have more
difficulty doing.

All of this has been said before, and with one exception I pretend no addition here to the immense legal scholarship that has
compared the civil law and common law over time. But there is
one consideration that I don't believe has received the attention it
deserves, it having to do, of course, with cognitions. Even with its
flexibility, the common law lawyer is overwhelmingly bound to
some adaptation of legal precedent within a contemporary legal
argument. That reasoning, invariably, is analogical, that is to say
linear in the sense that an almost syllogistic proof carries the burden of the common law's legal discovery. The rub is that the common law almost invariably affords a multiplicity of possible
precedents, quantitative research showing that ideology is the principal determinant of which precedent is chosen. In short, there is
a lot less ballast to the common law than what might first appear.
There is no necessary external reference to a more deeply based
principal, something that might come historically from a Ham-

murabi, a Justinian, or, with Napoleon, the *Code Civil* in the continental tradition. Neither is there a philosophical perspective that is, mercifully, less malleable. As a result, just as there is little of the dialectic in English or American philosophy, so too there is little of pure reason in the philosophically rich sense within the English jurisprudential tradition. Where the civil law employs philosophical reason, the common law depends on reason*ing*, in the calculus-based sense of that term, again with the risk of the ideologically laden choice. There is a great difference between reason and reasoning, and that difference has a good deal to do with cognitive forms, realizing, of course, that there are different philosophical perspectives as well as different interpretations of each philosophical perspective. But, at the least, there is a deeper grounding within a philosophically based perspective, and I would argue there is a better chance to have a balance of cognitive perspectives there.

To put a fine point on it, though a reliance on the internal calculus of the precedent-guided common law decision may still work well within the mother country, with its well-ordered social norms and its long history of a firm social order, the irony of the American version of the common law is that the freedom provided by the internal calculus of law does not ensure either legal precision or legal equity. The sad fact is that the linearity of analytic reasoning in the American law brings a greater, not a lesser variance of decision within a country like the United States than there is in a country like England. The absence of philosophical direction that results from a centuries old English tradition of "custom and usage," as Glanville, Bracton, Fortescue, Coke, Blackstone, and so many others understood it, and even the "experience" that America's O. W. Holmes, Jr. wrote of so eloquently, has still resulted in cases like *Dred Scott v. Sandford* (1857), the outrageous sanctification of slavery, *Santa Clara County v. Southern Pacific Railroad* (1886), which artificially personified a corporation in a way that, today, girds the oligarchy, *Korematsu v. The United States* (1944), wherein America brutally discriminated against a peoples whom recent evidence shows were even less of a danger than their defenders believed then, and, of course, *Buckley v. Valeo* (1976) and *Citizens United v. F.E.C.* (2010), wherein the corporations fully extended Santa Clara's outrage to the most precious of democratic freedoms: the right of a citizenry democratically to choose its political leadership. If you will, look *through* the written decisions of these atrocious cases. Are there cognitive balances in the tortured reasoning of Chief Justices Taney, or Roberts, or even in the good faith "split the difference" opinion of Justice Lewis Powell in *Buckley*? No, these cases all lack any semblance of cognitive balance. They are without philosophical grounding of any kind. In each awful case, the calculus of reasoning, not reason, lead a capricious court to inequitable findings. Incidentally, for my conservative friends, I will gladly throw out the bone that though I fervently endorse what the Earl Warren Court did in so many important legal areas, many of the opinions of a liberal justice like William O. Douglas also reflected the "looseness" of English common law reasoning in the American legal domain. Douglas's late career opinions were hopelessly ungrounded, if not outright unlegal.

So just as there has been little of the dialectic in English philosophy, Locke never tying his understanding of simple and complex cognitions to the dialectic for example, so too there has been no balance of cognitive forms within the English law, although the English, once again, have always had a well ordered society where "custom and usage" at least meant something to them. Why has it been that no one, whether Prof. Obama at the University of Chicago Law School or anyone else teaching at America's best law schools, has ever questioned why it is that the extraordinarily important, sole American dialectic-initiating case of *Shelley v. Kraemer* might import something beyond being a Fourteenth Amendment open housing case? The answer, I submit, is that even the best American law schools teach no more than analytically-formed, analogical precedent, ignoring the possibility of philosophically-based, cognitively balanced and at least partially synthetic, understandings. The progress of America's law, if increasingly corporate friendly Supreme Court rulings can be called progress, is not even up to the synthetic *a priori* limitations on knowledge (Chapter Eight), much less to the simultaneous balance between *a priori* analytic and synthetic forms of knowledge that, as I argued earlier, goes beyond Hegel's synthetic preference.

Ask a simple question: Did the very best of America's constitutional scholars, Akhil Reed Amar at Yale, Laurence Tribe at Harvard, or, say, Dick Howard at Virginia, ever write about the Constitution, the principal legal document of our nation, in the context of the pyramid of knowledge's apex point, or the forms? To my knowledge, they have not. I wrote of it some years ago, but why has it been that a sub-field like law, and law is only a sub-field like economics and political science do not forget, lost all contact with the queen discipline, philosophy, and the balances that exist at the top of the knowledge pyramid? The best American law schools simply don't teach that.

Please do not misunderstand. In many ways, I hold the English common law, and an education in that law such as I received, in high esteem. Once more, it has often lent a necessary flexibility to the American political/legal system as it has to other common law systems throughout the world. But, if one is to discover the deepest meanings of the law, and if one is to permit if not encourage the just, modern adaptations of something like the principles of equity that reside in Article III of the American Constitution as well as the equity-based jury prerogatives of the Seventh Amendment, principles transcending reasoning and aspiring to the best of reason as an aggregate of differentiated cognitive perspectives must be available. That is more of a civil law than a common law notion, but it is what is so glaringly missing in the American law school curriculum, as well as in the corridors of America's governments and its courts that are overwhelmingly dominated by common law lawyers.

The Second Suggestion — Amendments

My second suggestion revolves around the rebalancing of the political system itself. As I mentioned above (Chapter Twelve), the early 1980s saw a group of outstanding citizens gather into what they came to call The Committee on the Constitutional System. As earlier, I had a small hand in the creation of that group, calling for its assembling in my 1980 South Carolina Senate campaign and being responded to in *The New Republic* (March 8, 1980) and *The Christian Science Monitor* (February 26, 1980) by the dean of American political journalists, Richard Strout. Once more, CCS was principally chaired by Lloyd Cutler, who had served as counsel to the president under Jimmy Carter and was soon to do so for a short time in the Clinton administration. Former Treasury Secretary C. Douglas Dillon, and Senator Nancy Kassebaum (R-KS) also served as co-chairs, CCS proceeding to bring together what I believe to be the finest assemblage of A-list private citizens to discuss the Constitution in the history of the Republic. It did so in the run-up to the constitutional bicentennial, and presented America with its recommendations in January of 1987. Front page coverage was awarded in *The New York Times*. Full page coverage was granted by *The Washington Post*.

Though CCS developed several proposals for the improvement of our government, both constitutional and sub-constitutional, by far the most salient suggestion, again, was to extend the House of Representatives term from two years to four years, that term to run concurrently with the presidential term and, of course, necessitating resignation from the House if a member wished to run for the Senate in the interim election. This amendment would at least to some degree permit the citizenry to "form a government," as Lloyd Cutler liked to put it. It would mean that by electing a four-year president, a four-year lower house of the Congress as well as one-third of the upper house, there would be something of a mandate from the citizenry along with a configuration of political power that could carry out that mandate. Of course, this would still leave our system a long way from the typical European parliamentary system, but then CCS's members specifically eschewed the notion of parliamentary government for America, in what I recall was a very brief discussion. The four-year House term innovation would facilitate decision-making in the legislative branch, and at least partially inoculate the Congress from the excessive interest group influence that has for too long been a part of what is properly labeled as the "permanent campaign." What was the response of the

Democratic Party and its office-holders to even CCS' single core recommendation? Nothing. Absolutely nothing, and I have not forgotten that.

Secondarily, with regard to constitutional reform, I like many Americans have seen more than enough of the Electoral College. As many citizens know, three presidents have now been elected when someone else received a larger popular vote, Al Gore receiving 540,000 more votes than George W. Bush in 2000. Moreover, the lay of the political land among the so-called red, blue, and now modishly labeled purple states means that, at most, ten states are in play during the presidential campaign. This not only means that those states receive a highly disproportionate share of the campaigning by the presidential candidates but, even more importantly, that the citizens of the other states have no decisional power whatsoever in the outcome. Why should they vote? Because of the Electoral College, their vote doesn't count. The result of their state's vote is a foregone conclusion and, in many cases, the citizens of those states don't vote because they know the conclusion. This must change.

Third, I return to our earlier discussion of the Seventh Amendment, the core provision of the Bill of Rights regarding the tension between debtors and creditors, and the absolute necessity to enact campaign finance legislation. The simplest amendment, making it clear that the large contribution is not protected under the first amendment, that it is in fact a contract or an understanding that a specific return is anticipated for a specific, large contribution is necessary if anything like a representative democracy is to survive. The amount can be set by the Congress, but all bundling, and other duplicitous guises for large interest contributions, must be banned beyond that figure.

There are somewhat lesser innovations that should receive at least some consideration by the American people and their political leaders. I'll mention but three here. First, I subscribe to the efforts of the former Wisconsin Democratic Senator Russ Feingold regarding the requirement for an election rather than a gubernatorial appointment in the selection of a Senator who fills a vacant seat. The embarrassing chicanery that accompanied the appointment of my home state's junior senator in 2008, Roland Burris (D-IL), reminded us again that the Seventeenth Amendment's popularization of the Senatorial vote fell short of assuring that the people's wishes would be paramount in Senatorial replacements, as they are in House replacements.

Secondly, and not included in the recommendations of CCS incidentally, I have come to the conclusion that the vice-president, whoever she or he may be, must now serve only at the pleasure of the president. Ideology aside, what went on between George W. Bush and Dick Cheney in the last year of the Bush presidency, with their relationship deteriorating and the Condoleezza Rice/Robert Gates replacement of Cheney as a trusted adviser and Donald Rumsfeld as Secretary of Defense, must never be allowed to happen again. When liberals are finished with harpooning our last president, let us at least award a half point to the younger Bush for his refusal to pardon the vice president's chief of staff, the lying-under-oath Scooter Libby. Libby, thanks to the federal attorney Pat Fitzgerald, went to jail.

The sad fact is that the recent vice-president's last days' ranting about his office being partly of the executive branch and partly of the legislative branch had far more constitutional substance to it than liberals, and particularly the liberal press, wanted to acknowledge. The vice-presidency, we should not forget, was the silver medal in the original presidential Olympics. We should not forget either that the prerogative of breaking ties was far more meaningful when there were but twenty-six senators (actually twenty-four—Rhode Island not being at the Convention and an iffy joiner of the union) being the number the framers were working with - not the current one hundred. That America's principal political divide was already the regional separation between North and South (New Jersey being the "border" state) made the tie breaking power even more meaningful. Being head of the Senate was not an inconsequential compensation for a political figure, even if that individual had not been a part of the presidential sweepstakes. The office remains unchanged in the Constitution.

What Cheney threatened may have been the greatest challenge to the prerogatives of the executive branch, if not the entire constitutional order, in the history of the Republic. What if the split had happened years earlier, when Cheney was in better health and still far more plugged in to the labyrinth of Washington power centers than the younger Bush ever was? Though neither principal may ever deign to talk about it, Cheney's position was nothing short of a threat, directed not at all at liberal control of the Senate. It was leveled at the president, whom he felt he could intimidate into a Libby pardon by holing up in a bunker at the other end of Pennsylvania Ave. More significantly, it was leveled at the presidency itself. The vice presidency must no longer remain *sui juris*.

Finally, among lesser but still important changes, I recommend what I mentioned before, that is the federal limiting of outrageous ballot access hurdles for federal offices that have been enacted by so many states. The Democrats can blame Ralph Nader for what happened in 2000 all they like, but to have had the third highest presidential vote getter in 2000 and 2004 be excluded from the ballots of five American states in 2008 is a blatant example of state's wrongs. Can anyone name a democratic nation-state in Europe, or even countries like Australia or Canada, wherein a national sub-jurisdiction, something like a German lander or a Canadian province, can exclude the third most prominent national office seeker for the highest office in the land? The ballot access threshold for presidential, senatorial, and representative candidates of any party should never exceed one percent of a state's vote for that office in the previous election. If this takes a constitutional amendment so be it, although legislation may be sufficient. It is the will, from the two corporate dominated parties, that is lacking.

Please recall that during the Progressive era in the early years of the twentieth century, three significant amendments, the Sixteenth that initiated the progressive income tax, the Seventeenth that brought about the popular vote for Senators, and the Nineteenth that gave women the vote, made the most significant, and democratic, changes to our constitutional order since the founding. What if a) the four year House term, b) the eradication of the Electoral College and c) the amending of the Constitution to permit real campaign finance reform, served as a triad of twenty-first century progressive politics that would both strengthen the government at the same time that it afforded greater accountability of that government to its people? And what if we threw in the Senatorial vacancy election, vice-presidential service at the presidential will, and reasonable ballot access for federal offices? And if we truly wished to be bold, we should at least consider proportional representation, non-partisan district drawing, and either instant run-off or rank ordering voting as well. Then, maybe, we would have true reform within the American political system. As an aside, I also advocate, although legislation on the matter is not possible, that all responses to telephone, email, and other communications regarding a citizen's voting preference for candidates be dishonest. When these people call you, either refuse to tell them whom you are voting for or just lie. Forcing candidates to tell you what they believe without a Dick Morris poll in front of them would improve government greatly.

I close this subsection with the simplest of reminders. It is that in our country's two most recent economic tights, it has not been the constitutional institutions that got us out of the mess. It was Paul Volcker and the Feds who stanched inflation with the painful but necessary crunching of high interest rates in the Carter/Reagan period and it was Ben Bernanke and the Feds who have at least partially bailed us out of the Great Recession. Even liberal economists like Paul Krugman concede that the Obama $787.2 billion stimulus was not adequate. It was all our constitutional system would permit.

A Third Suggestion —
A Green Global Party

Beyond the amending of the Constitution in such a way as to rebalance the analytic-to-synthetic forms within our governmental structures, there is one sub-constitutional innovation that I also believe to be central to the improvement of our government. I discussed the importance of building a trans-national, even global, political party in Chapter Fourteen and will not revisit that general argument here. But let me be specific. The fact is that the Green

Party is now the largest party in the world, measured by the number of countries we are in. In 2008, eighty-three of the world's eighty-eight Green parties met at a global conference in Sao Paulo, Brazil. Now we are up to ninety-three, with other, larger meetings following Sao Paulo. As I've mentioned, the Democratic Party has done nothing to create, or even be a part of, a global political party of the non-totalitarian left. Let us now fill that void. With the default of the Big Box parties, let us urge the Greens to be the cutting edge of creating a truly global party.

Please recall my earlier discussion on the cognitive forms of various global institutions, including the forms of the private sector institutions, which are invariably analytic. Are we not now obligated to counterbalance those institutions? I think so. Yes, the current president is up to his elbows with a nagging economic recovery, wars that don't go away, the immigration crisis, the energy crisis, the environment, and so on. But I have heard nothing of global institution building, even in his usually lofty campaign speeches. But think: it might have been convenient, mightn't it, if trans-national parties had been available to help deal with something like the current global economic crisis, and maybe even global warming, and global health issues, and, yes, even the wars.

Today, this synthetic institutional linkage is not available. Perhaps, when the rain stops falling on the roof, the now far less than new American president may see it to be in our country's interest to support the one institution, even beyond something like the United Nations, that might have the most beneficial impact on the world. But, again, nothing in his background or record demonstrates even an interest in doing something like this. Meanwhile, the Green Party is growing in its global reach and it will continue to do so. Maybe the Greens will become the first truly global party. Maybe we should all support a Green Party that would help realize the vision of those like Richard Falk and the others like myself and Prof. Kegley who have written of a new global order.

Why did I join the Green Party? Please permit a moment of personal history. One of my great grandfathers was the president of the Chicago Grocers and Butchers Association, over one hundred years ago. A great uncle was the Chicago city auditor, from 1927 to

1957. One grandfather was a principal aide to Anton Cermak and my father was the first president of the Chicago Police Board, he receiving the first phone call from Mayor Richard J. Daley after the 1960 Richard Morrison "babbling burglar" police scandal. The mayor asked my father to become chief, but he turned it down and suggested the creation of a civilian board to oversee and reform a corrupt department.

My mother was very much of an Illinois Whig, a follower of the Lincoln tradition running up through figures like Wendell Wilkie. *One World* was obligatory reading in our home. I can still remember telling my mother (when I taught for two years at The University of Tennessee) how Pauline Gore (wife of Senator Al Gore, Sr.) had gone to law school in the nineteen-thirties, and receiving "Son, have you forgotten who went to law school in the 1920s?" Yes, mother. She was extraordinarily well read, having worked as a librarian in the Chicago Public Library for many years and her reverence for Abraham Lincoln did not prevent her from voting for good Democratic liberals like Franklin Roosevelt, Harry Truman, and even Hubert Humphrey a good while later.

But perhaps most fortunately, there was a third strand to my political socialization, great figures from the Upper Midwest including Robert LaFollette that I wrote of earlier being approvingly introduced to me by my father, whose first year of college, at The University of Wisconsin, was 1923–1924. There was something about Upper Midwestern politics that included an understanding of the balances of the private and the public sectors, and the obligation of the public sector to ensure a minimum safety net for its citizens, that both my parents spoke of with reverence. My parents were hardly socialists, but the term, particularly as it was used in the context of those Wisconsin city governments that existed during my childhood, was not a dirty word.

My own first experience with meaningful national politics came at the Fontainebleau Hotel in Miami Beach, FL, in the summer of 1972, after working on counter-drafts of a proposed constitution for the Democratic Party since the fall of 1971. It was the Mc-Governites' convention, and they had included a New Left inspired charter for consideration in their constitutional draft that sported a 2,000-person national committee, a rule that members of the executive committee could not come from the regular committee, and a collage of other bizarre impediments to effective political activity. I listened long enough to the polite members of the team that argued ineffectively with Rep. Donald Fraser (D-MN)—the other half of the McGovern-Fraser Commission that had created this monstrosity. Then I broke in. "Hey, Congressman: have you ever run a meeting with 2,000 people?" Getting his attention, though he did not say anything, I followed up with "Hey, Congressman: if the executive committee and the full committee can't have the same people on them, who's in charge?" Noting that the congressman's attention level had improved considerably, I closed with "What are you trying to do, ruin the Democratic Party?" Three hours later, a McGovern minion called the South Carolina office to announce the withdrawing of the charter from the convention agenda. Over the next two years, my draft was the working document of the Terry Sanford-led Commission that wrote a sensible constitution for the Democratic Party. I am the principal drafter of that document.

Shortly thereafter, noting as above that the same problems that the McGovern-Fraser draft charter evidenced had infected Congressional Democrats in their 1975 disassembling of the United States Congress, I took leave without pay from the University of South Carolina and entered the 1980 South Carolina Senatorial primary in order to discuss the issue of governmental fragmentation. I predicted then that the government would no longer be able to control the federal deficit. I also predicted that gridlock would become the norm within both the interaction of the Congress with the presidency and within and between the two congressional houses. At that moment, the debt was $942 billion, and the annual deficit $63 billion. In 1984, I took LWOP again, entering the New Hampshire presidential primary and giving forums at twenty-two colleges and universities throughout New England and upstate New York. Faculty members such as Lester Thurow and Bruce Mazlich joined our panel at M.I.T. Don Robinson at Smith College participated, inviting William College's James MacGregor Burns to join us there. I was summoned to Montana for three days by a constitutional reformer there, garnering a few votes in that state's Democratic convention. The press was kind to me throughout the campaign.

In the spring of 1992, I took LWOP one more time and gave forums from Haverford College in Philadelphia, PA down to The Thomas Jefferson Society at The University of Virginia. I gathered a few votes in the South Carolina presidential primary where I campaigned but little, at least finishing ahead of Lyndon LaRouche and some others. In the year 2000, I entered the South Carolina Democratic Party caucuses, intentionally violating three FEC regulations in the hopes of getting a test case that would challenge the *Buckley* ruling. They didn't bite. The FEC didn't want to give me a forum, but the late Molly Ivins and others liked what I was doing, and wrote about it. In each of these campaigns, I discussed not only undemocratic decentralization but the growing ineffectiveness and interest group-led infection of the government. I led Al Gore for the fifth delegate in the second congressional district in South Carolina after the precinct round before throwing in. The Democratic Party paid no attention and I slowly removed myself from it. But the Democratic Party's wholesale ignoring of the pleas of good citizens for structural change in our government was not the only reason I left. There were three other reasons.

The first reason concerned the corporations. In 2002, witnessing the pillage of the poor state of South Carolina by the newly interstate Charlotte banks, I agreed to become the campaign manager for a third party congressional candidate named Mark Whittington. Whittington ran for Congress in the same South Carolina congressional district where I had received some presidential support two years earlier, he receiving over 10% of the vote. We got those votes largely because Whittington, I, and eight other South Carolinians picketed the national headquarters of the Bank of America on the corner of Trade and Tryon Streets in Charlotte, NC. Our principal banner read "Charlotte Banks Bleed South Carolina." Local citizens stopped to talk with us, telling us that their state suffered from BOA's predatory lending as well.

For his outspokenness, Whittington was dismissed from his job, having to borrow money from his friends to feed his family. I continued to speak out on the outrages within the financial service sector, but leading Democrats seemed to believe that the issue was unimportant and continued cashing contribution checks from the banks. The increasingly cozy relationship that the Democratic Party had developed with the corporations, particularly the financial service corporations, was one of the principal reasons I left the Democratic Party. And, don't forget, the major parties were still taking money from a bank that we now understand was not only not processing the loan modifications that it claimed it was processing but was in fact paying bonuses to employees who foreclosed on loans, throwing people out of their homes. I put it simply. If the Democrats had supported what ten of us South Carolinians picketed for that day, there would have been no Global Recession.

Regarding Whittington, I should add that after attending college for one year, long before his campaign, Mark decided he could do better educating himself. A true autodidact, he continued reading and learning, a process he continues to this day while working as both an electrician and, more recently, a computer programmer with his own small company. He reads theory, and tinkers with a theory of his own. Mark helps to remind me that the conventional mind, the analytic mind, simply cannot engage in the early detection of that alteration of form that makes up the second, synthetic, stage of the dialectic. It was an honor to be a manager of a small campaign that had little money but that took a video of our picketing of the Bank of America, and showed it on five cable channels in and around Columbia, SC, in 2002. That's how a lefty broke ten percent of the vote in a South Carolina congressional district. The incumbent we ran against, incidentally, was Joe "you lie" Wilson who, as above, embarrassed our country before the world with his State of the Union outcry. Mr. Whittington's United Citizens Party, now defunct with many of its members joining the Greens, is in Wikipedia. I will say it again: if the Democratic Party had taken the position that the ten of us took in the fall of 2002, there would have been no Global Recession.

Secondly, I left the Democratic Party because of its relationship to the Abrahamic Civil War. As a Taoist, much influenced by the Baha'i religion because of my birth and rearing near their Wilmette, Illinois Mother Temple, I understood but was increasingly impatient with the advocacy of so many of America's Christians, Muslims, and Jews in what was ultimately their uncivil conflict. More importantly, as an American who never rang a doorbell to support a political candidate with the thought of any other country in mind, I could no longer abide the divided national loyalties of so many significant contributors to the Democratic Party. But let me be clear; though I have no doubt that the Israeli lobby has done great harm to our country, I have no illusion that the Arab/Muslim lobby would not have done every bit as much harm, and encouraged similar divided loyalties, if it had had the ability to do so. I have been even-handed in the Abrahamic Civil War. It must stop, and those of us who are outside of the Abrahamic faiths must no longer shy away from being active, unabashedly critical, parts of the solution.

Incidentally, I am hardly the first to say that the Christian fundamentalists have also had far too much sway in the Republican Party. They burden those of us of no divided national loyalties with the all too often warlike opinions of those who do. In fairness, it must be said that some in the Green Party have a tilt to them, they being anti-Israeli. My parents' teachings about religious tolerance, and my early identity with the marvelous Baha'i religion that has its international headquarters safely havened in Haifa, have kept me from having preferences in what is misnamed the Middle East conflict. How about getting it right, and calling it what it is? How about calling it the Abrahamic Civil War, the unwelcome product of the violent extremes that exist within all three Abrahamic faiths, those extremes also being the catalyst to so many intra-faith conflicts, like the Shiite-Sunni conflicts, and the religious versus secular conflicts that increasingly bedevil the Islamic, Christian, and Jewish worlds? Note that the religious/secular conflict now reflects the very psychological differentiation that we reviewed in Chapter Fifteen. My thanks, of course, to the brave handful of clerics and lay people on all sides who have accepted responsibility for trying to end the religiously generated violence. They have genuinely attempted to broker understandings amongst the parties, but their efforts have thus far not stopped the violence.

So I left the Democratic Party, in addition to the corporate linkages, because both the Republican and Democratic parties have all too frequently engaged in the kind of political activity that reflects a) the violation of the first tenet of the Judeo-Christian Decalogue, b) the violation of the admonitions against serving two masters as in the English common law of agency, and c) George Washington's admonition against "passionate attachments" to other countries, as I mentioned in an earlier chapter. It is they who bear responsibility for the fact that those of us Americans who have no divided national loyalties have endured seeing our country harmed by those who do. I have witnessed far too many instances of both Republican and Democratic candidates for public office not speaking out about the Abrahamic Civil War because what they might say would find them being called anti-Semitic by the lobby. I have seen far too many instances of good American citizens who were intimidated out of expressing themselves in their own country for fear of being slandered as a bigot. That slander, and the fear of it, has worked for the lobby, and it is a good part of the reason for why we still are where we are in that conflict.

But there is a third reason for why I left the Democratic Party, something that deals with what I have written of throughout this work. It is the deep bias of temperament that exists within that party, as well as most of American politics. I have no doubt that that bias is what underlay the ignoring, and in some cases ridiculing, of efforts such as my own concerning the deep structural imbalances of our government, I immodestly having been proven right about such things as our institutional gridlock, the enormous national debt, as well as the outrageous conduct of America's financial institutions. At the highest level of abstraction, at the level that deals with the *forms* of knowledge, the placement of those forms within the cognitive preferences of real citizens, and the role of those forms in both the maintenance of an equitable society and a society that is capable of transcending the historical dialectic, the American Democratic Party increasingly became a disappointment for me. As I've said, no one of genuine theoretical or artistic credentials holds an important position in the Democratic Party.

What I ask, therefore, is that we look at the crises that our country and our world now faces, and examine not just their substance but their forms. It is the synthetic cognition, is it not, that has been missing in the lack of care for the environment? It is the synthetic cognition that has been missing in our casual involvement in avoidable wars. It is the synthetic cognition that has been missing in the understanding of the American government's budget and trade deficits. It is the synthetic cognition that has been missing in the thus far failed solutions to the immigration conundrum. It is the synthetic cognition that has been missing in the decline of our infrastructure. It is the absence of the synthetic cognition that has allowed the food industry to implant ingredients like high fructose corn syrup into the foods that have led to Type I diabetes cases among our young, and permitted the harm of other additives such as Monsanto's GMOs. It is the synthetic cognition that has never succeeded in counterbalancing bilateral, contractually formed, lobbying and campaign activities that continue to prostitute our government. Finally, it is the absence of the synthetic cognition that has divorced the barest considerations of equity from the everyday employment contracts of too many working Americans.

The New Iron Triangle

Change will not be easy. Fundamental political change, perhaps more than any other alteration, never is. But let us understand what the greatest impediment to fundamental change is, I believing that a new constellation of structural barriers stands in our way. With the deepest respect for the writings of Cornell University's Theodore Lowi and his pre-sub-atomic Iron Triangle of American politics of forty years ago that indicted interest groups, legislators, and administrative agencies in the context of their collective harm to our country, I suggest that a new, sub-atomically rooted Iron Triangle now threatens our political system still further. The Lowi Iron Triangle described the back-scratching relationships of interest groups, members of Congress within their interest group "accessed" committees and sub-committees, and the regulatory agencies that he claimed had been cornered and "captured" by the interests. The money, the contractually formed understandings, and the gathering routinization of their incestuous relationships tied the system into mutually beneficial procedural knots. The public sector's common will was habitually thwarted while the private sector's singular wills were invariably served.

At its core, the new, sub-atomic Iron Triangle I suggest has come into existence exposes the inaccurate belief that the internal calculus of the electoral cycle guarantees the maintenance of a general political equilibrium, as well as the fairness and workability of the American system. The fact is that no internal calculus, of any system, ever guarantees general equilibrium. A perfectly functioning watch does not guarantee that the time on its face is accurate. The new, sub-atomic Iron Triangle is, as we would expect, purely analytic in its cognitive form. Its adherents claim that no external equilibriation, no consideration beyond the playing out of the by now highly routinized secular political mass, is needed. They say that because their own minds are incapable of abstracting beyond the analytic forms of the electoral calculus, and because the electoral calculus is literally swimming in money.

What should the components of the sub-atomic Iron Triangle be? The first leg, I suggest, is made up of the major party candidates, each of whom (including the current president) have scrupulously avoided discussion of fundamental political change. The second and third legs of the new Iron Triangle are made up of a) the campaign industry and b) the political journalists, both of whom are obsessed with the next election and the obligatory story line that the next election might bring an upturn in the nation's fortunes with the reduction of the deficits, the trade imbalances, the increasingly disastrous income and wealth distributions, and so on. The Jim Carville/Karl Rove kind of campaign industry complicity, along with their horse race-dictated candidate and election commentary, insists upon the singular importance of the immediate political context, and the sterile interpretations that they alone give to it. These gatekeepers for the American electoral system, all of whom receive a pretty nickel for their concentration on the most immediate and most temporary of campaign issues, have falsely represented that America's problems are not systemic. It is these campaign industry oligarchs who have also represented that their level of political understanding is the highest level of understanding available and that listening to them and their candidates alone will lead to the surest political solutions.

As for the commentators, even an otherwise knowledgeable MSNBC-TV correspondent like Chris Matthews emphatically preaches the idiosyncratic doctrine of politics with no patterns, and little linkage between our country's political issues and those far larger issues that surround the working of the political system itself. Do Matthews and his similarly disposed colleagues not see the vapid repetitiveness of the American campaign ritual? Do they not see that false banalities like his oft-repeated Tip O'Neill mantra that "all politics is local" are so intellectually confining that, at best, they only mask the outrageous distributionally unjust character of our government that began to appear in the 1970s and accelerated in the Reagan/Tip O'Neill years? After all, it was 1981, with its new income tax schedule, and 1983, with its deficit reduction plan that laid the burden for revenue regeneration on the highly regressive payroll tax that Alan Greenspan insisted on, that initiated the current redistributional avalanche. All politics is local could not be a more cognitively analytic claim, rivaled only in error in the entire second half of the twentieth century by the mantra of the Democratic President John F. Kennedy that "a rising tide lifts all boats," virtually all of the last forty years proving that banality to be wholly unfounded.

Politics, which Albert Einstein properly judged to be more difficult than physics, is a delicate and deliciously complex mixture of the local and the non-local, as well as the distributionally fair and the distributionally unfair, both things being much better understood in at least some other countries. True enough, there is something of the local in all politics, but that is as far from understanding the long peace among the centuries-old conflicting nations of Europe, the American-led political and military alliance that beat Hitler and Tojo, the collapse of the Soviet Empire, and the modern rise of the Confucian and Taoist notions that, in spite of a government unsympathetic to their teachings, subtly underpinned so much of the most dramatic elevation of fortune in all of economic history: modern China. It almost goes without saying that the sub-atomic Iron Triangle, once more made up of a) the political candidate, b) the campaign industry, and c) the commentary of an increasingly near-sighted media, is now every bit as damaging to our nation as Prof. Lowi's pre-sub-atomic triangle was in its time. The cyclically bounded candidates, the enriched campaign industry oligarchs, and the Dostoyevskian Grand Interpreters, have contributed mightily, if not magnanimously, to our political decline. Would it ever be possible, for example, that mechanics like Carville and Rove, or commentators like MSNBC's Matthews and FOX's Sean Hannity, might decide that for one election cycle, or even one day, they would step outside their lucrative commentary on ever more dilatory campaigns and speak to the deep structural problems of our country's government? I doubt it. Like the other members of the sub-atomic Iron Triangle, the money, the limelight, and the false sense of political omniscience, all cloak the intellectual inability to create, much less relate, any depth of political understanding. For those like them, relentless attacks on the notion that there are patterns in politics, as the classical theorists like Plato, Aristotle, and the German Idealists like Kant and Hegel so clearly understood, was simply too irresistible. Their world, which they gratuitously share with us, is purely of the spontaneous, the idiosyncratic, and ultimately the uninformed and the unformed. Is it possible that, not unlike the transformative paradigm shift of the philosophical and jurisprudential fission-fusion, and the religious paradigm shift from having the principal variance exist within the pagan faiths to across all faiths, the real political divide in American politics is between the technocratic accomplices of both parties on one side, and the scholars who have argued that the political system has become dysfunctional and the knowledgeable citizenry that knows they're right on the other?

In sum, assisted to be sure by the Lyndon Johnson "unified budget" of 1969 that conveniently masked the daunting deficits and growing debt, the conventional minds behind America's all too conventional politics not only did not mitigate the deep cognitive imbalances that have unstructured our country's politics; they exacerbated them. So if we are properly to include what has heretofore been excluded, let me reiterate that it is time for a new political perspective, a transcendent, integrative cross-weave of a political theory that is based, as I've suggested, on cognitions generally, and more specifically on the unrelenting American political bias against the synthetic cognition and those personalities that manifest the synthetic cognition. Perhaps for the future, in the bargain, our country could avoid those like the Clinton presidency's deregulating Treasury Secretary Robert Rubin who, at the time of his retirement as head of Wall Street's Goldman Sachs, uttered an insouciant little comment about how he "didn't know how the private sector could go so haywire." Well, some knowledgeable, and courageous, citizens did know, Bob. Mr. Whittington knew how the private sector could go haywire. Mr. Whittington sacrificed in the early telling of that reality to the citizens of both South and North Carolina, an electrician stepping into the political world, speaking truth to his fellow Americans. And if the Republicans and Democrats intractably wish to repeat the sobriquet about third parties being "spoilers" that harm the ideologically proximate candidate, let them remember Mr. Whittington, when both Big Box parties were taking money from the banks and there was no choice among them that would have prevented either the predatory lending or the building of the economic bubble that burst into the Great Recession. That's what third parties are for, and what third parties have done throughout American history, the major parties so often combining, just like Adam Smith's false economic competitors. Mr. Whittington is in good company.

One more point on political parties. One of the few happy signs of today's political world is the increasing number of American citizens who do not align with either one of the Big Box parties and consider themselves to be independents. This is so much the better for all of us, although it would be better still if more of these citizens actively supported a third party. You know my preference there. But short of that, for those who do not wish to work in a new and challenging party, let me suggest a more moderate and perhaps more realizable goal. What if a large number of the citizens who still wished to identify with the Democrats and Republicans were far more willing, when state law allowed it, to cross over in the primary voting that so often precedes general elections, such voting frequently determining the eventual winner in the election? It is far too common for Republican and Democratic Party activists to recommend either not crossing over at all to their flock, thereby permitting an unqualified, and often more extreme candidate, to win the other major party's nomination (and possibly winning the general election) or, worse, crossing over only to strike down the more qualified candidate of the other party in the hope of defeating the less qualified candidate in the general election. Well, this strategy works sometimes, but when it doesn't, America pays with unqualified, ideologically extreme officials.

Let me share three examples about why this overdone loyalty to party can be so harmful. All these examples are from the recent political history of the state of South Carolina. To begin, let us recall that Democrats still pretend that Ralph Nader cost Al Gore the presidency in the year 2000. Apart from the fact that Gore's lawyer, who was expelled from his first law school, failed to ask for a recount of all Florida counties rather than just four counties, and apart from the fact that this same lawyer didn't say a word when a Supreme Court justice asked "what would you have us do?" during oral argument, the obvious answer being "continue the count," the election may in fact have been lost, or at a minimum the lesser Republican was catapulted to the front ahead of John McCain when almost no South Carolina Democrats crossed over and voted in the Republican primary. As a result, the nation got W, and this when Bill Bradley had dropped out of the Democratic race and Vice President Gore was opposed only by a plucky political science professor who had intentionally violated a number of F.E.C. regulations in order to prompt a case that would challenge *Buckley v. Valeo* and its progeny. This failure to cross over is the result of a phenomenon called E.P.I. — Excessive Party Identification — and the above example is but one of many, this placing the worst candidate from both parties in high political office.

The second example involved the 2010 South Carolina gubernatorial election. Here too Democrats, who of course could still have voted for their candidate in the general election, did not cross over and vote for someone like the moderate Republican Attorney General Henry McMaster. As a result, a right-wing fanatic named Nikki Haley became the GOP nominee and, predictably, the governor. The most challenged citizens at the bottom of the pile in South Carolina suffer mightily, being excluded from the Medicaid option as of this writing because of this party-over-citizenry political choice. E.P.I. once more.

I should point out in this context that the moderate South Carolina Republican Senator Lindsey Graham will be up for reelection in 2014. Republican Tea Party candidates are already picking up where the Democrats' last campaign against him ended, Graham's sexual preference being the focus of these efforts. Do you think that some South Carolina Democrats could cross over and vote in the primary for an intelligent and "willing to bargain" Senator from the "other" party, or would it be too much to ask to put country first? The likelihood of Democrats winning this Senate seat in 2014 is slim, although Democrats will be free to compete vigorously against Senator Graham in November.

The point could not be simpler. The same kinds of analytic minds that are not able to extend their thinking beyond the immediate campaign calculus, the minds whose political universe is never more than the battle between the current prostitutions of Lincoln and Wilkie and the current contradictions of Jefferson and Roosevelt, are the very kinds of minds that consistently demonstrate an inability to rise above the immediate partisan cause and defeat the candidate, regardless of party, who would do the most harm to our country. The damage that these minds have caused over the last decades results not only from their parties' candidates and office holders; it results as well from the Democratic and Republican Parties' campaign industry mediocrities, their limitations being ratified unfortunately by an all too partisan citizenry. The founders of our country did not include political parties in the Constitution for a reason. Though undoubtedly necessary today, excessive identification with any one of them does precisely what those founders who feared parties were concerned about. We suffer from E.P.I.

In closing this work, I return simply to Bohr and Rutherford, to Kant and Hegel, to Jung, to Barbara Ehrenreich and Susan Cain, and ultimately to my own sub-atomically-based theory, a theory created out of no more, but no less, than an understanding of the workings of different kinds of minds and the different philosophical and ultimately political positions these minds favor. All of the above, of course, also permit an understanding of the differentiated cognitions that reside within different political structures and processes. What the practitioners need to remember, and what they do remember when they take a sick child to a doctor expecting the most recent regimens of care to cure her, is that in any field those who do basic research invariably have deeper understandings than do the practitioners. It is true in medicine, physics, chemistry, biology, indeed all the disparate worlds of knowledge, and it is true in politics. The practitioners not only do not understand things like the bias of temperament; in fact, they ratify it. As a result of their bias, they have demonstrated neither the incentive nor the ability to correct the bias. It is only in one field, the field of politics, where the practitioners have the audacity to claim that they understand things better than those who do basic research. Well, they don't understand things better than those who do basic research, and they never have. The tragic evidence that they never have is available everywhere you look in American politics.

It is long overdue, therefore, to recognize the coming of the next historical stage, the stage of the Horizontal Revolution, or the time of a new form that Hegel properly understood as representing the next historical stage. This stage is a new order of the mind that accompanies the coming together of a new global reality. That kind of progression is invariably ushered into history as a product of the synthetic cognition, and so it will be with the next progression. The current president, Mr. Obama, marks the end of the departing historical stage, not a new beginning, as he and his followers falsely claim. He is at the end of the objectively based political paradigm, although we can hope that a woman will someday hold the presidential office. Please do not misunderstand; I originally wished the new president well. He is intelligent, if only in the conventional sense, and he is in his own way both earnest and disciplined. But the decline of the government itself, wholly apart from the failure of specific policies, has continued under this sixth president of my writing and politicking about our government's decline, just as it continued with the analytically biased failures of the fifth, fourth, third, second, and, of course, the first: the deregulating Jimmy Carter. Obama now complains of a worsening gridlock himself. Has he read the recommendations of CCS?

"There is not a liberal America and a conservative America." Did Barack Obama really say that? Is there no Black and White America, as Obama understood in his remarks about Trayvon Martin? Are there no women and men? Are there no gays and straights? Owners and workers? At the sub-atomic level, how do you balance the cognitions, and how do you utilize the synthetic cognition to transcend the dialectical contradiction, when you deny the critical cognitive distinction between different minds in the first place? The most important term, the term that Hegel used most pointedly throughout "The Idea of Cognition" chapter in his *Science of Logic*, was "difference," and Hegel was not referring to objective identity, or even policy, differentiations. His "difference" was of the forms, as introduced by Plato and as was so central to the epistemological commentary of those I have mentioned like Leonardo, Michelangelo, Malraux, and so many others.

Does Barack Obama understand it when it comes to temperament? The presidential candidate who asked America's citizenry to accept a difference that was greater than any political figure in American history, even greater than the Catholic John F. Kennedy, now denies the acceptance of difference to others? I have a problem with that. And if you are among those, like me, who believe that quiet, bi-partisan collusion between the analytic minds of both the Republican and Democratic party officials and the lucrative campaign industry, as above, has generated the ever more imbalanced policies of the recent political generation, much of it created from nothing more than what the anti-trust law calls the "conscious parallelism" of like-minded thinking, then a call for a false bi-partisanship doesn't cut it. Again I ask: what if the fission-fusion has now come to politics, beyond philosophy and jurisprudence, and if the true Grand Divide in American politics is between those who believe in the self-equilibriation of the sterile electoral calculus, both Democratic and Republican on one side, and those within the scholarly community and informed citizenry who understand that our entire political system is imbalanced and who therefore believe in the necessity for a cognitively synthetic restructuring of that system's structures and processes?

The irony here is that as the analytics see it, the government has worked very well, with a compromised and what they had hoped was an unconstitutional health care bill; a Swiss cheese, unraveling, Wall Street bill; the foot dragging on immigration; dealing only haltingly with the deficits; the snail-like progress of global warming solutions; not dealing with declining living standards for the average American; and not responding, at the philosophical and political levels, to the analytic minds in both parties who are responsible for so much of our inequitable, dilatory politics. Constitutional democracy is grounded in an appreciation of, and a balancing of, different interests and different perspectives, not a false unity that denies those differences. Abraham Lincoln understood that, but then Lincoln understood the dialectic. The Taoist yin and yang, of course, is grounded in it. The homogenization of differences violates my religion, Mr. President. But, more importantly, it violates my theory.

In the final analysis, this country only survives when it develops the same level of trust amongst people of different temperaments, conceptually on the horizontal, that it slowly and painfully learned to develop, vertically, concerning the inclusion of women, or African Americans, or any other pre-sub-atomic, undifferentiated objective groups in the polity. Only then will the temperaments be able to share political power, probably alternately, within a government that breaks through its gridlock and tacks its dialectical way through history, much as our parents told us to share with the siblings that we were quarreling with over toys, TV, and the attention of parents itself. But we will do this only when we see opposites as complements, as the Tao teaches, and acknowledge the varied subjectivities that rest within all objectivities, as I have tried to explain here. Until we do that, the public sector bias of temperament, like the private sector bias of temperament that Barbara Ehrenreich and Susan Cain have written about, will continue to bedevil us.

References

Abraham Lincoln, "Speech at Chicago, Illinois" in *Abraham Lincoln: Speeches and Writings,* Roy P. Basler, ed., New York, The Library of America, 1989, 315.

William P. Kreml, *The Twenty-First Century Left—Cognitions In The Constitution And Why* Buckley v. Valeo *Is Wrong,* Durham, Carolina Academic Press, 2006.

Wendell Wilkie, *One World,* New York, Simon and Schuster, 1943.

Dred Scott v. Sandford, 60 US (39 Howard) 393 (1857).

Erie v. Tompkins, 304 U.S. 64 (1938).

Korematsu v. U.S., 323 U.S. 214 (1944).

Santa Clara County v. Southern Pacific Railroad, 118 U. S. 394 (1886).

Citizens United v. F.E.C., 558 U. S. 08-208 (2010).

Index